Social Justice in Contemporary Housing

T0386329

Philosophy is not usually seen as a guidance for modern housing policy, but in this new book, Dr Helen Taylor argues that there is something innovative, unusual, and worth discussing about the application of philosophy to housing. The philosophical framework used within this book is John Rawls' conception of justice as fairness. The UK has gone through several shifts in housing policy over the past decade, most recently by introducing the controversial 'Bedroom Tax', in an effort to make more cuts to benefits and social welfare.

Social Justice in Contemporary Housing: Applying Rawls' Difference Principle suggests that by using ideas of agency, we can understand the impact that social policy has on individuals and wider society. The work outlines the liberal principle of legitimacy and argues that Rawls' concept of reasonableness can, and should, be used to justify the intervention of policy in individuals' lives. This book will be of interest to undergraduate and postgraduate students of housing as well as philosophy and social policy, and also those working around the creation and implementation of social housing in the UK.

Helen Taylor is a lecturer in housing studies at Cardiff Metropolitan University, UK. She is Communications Officer for the Housing Studies Association, as well as a board member for housing sector organisations Newport City Homes and Cymorth Cymru, and sector publication *Welsh Housing Quarterly*.

Routledge Focus on Housing and Philosophy

Routledge Focus offers both established and early-career academics the flexibility to publish cutting-edge commentary on topical issues, policy-focused research, analytical or theoretical innovations, in-depth case studies, or short topics for specialized audiences. The format and speed to market is distinctive. Routledge Focus are 20,000 to 50,000 words and will be published as eBooks, and in Hardback as print on demand.

This book series seeks to develop the links between housing and philosophy. It seeks proposals from academics and policy-makers on any aspect of philosophy and its relation to housing. This might include ethics, political and social philosophy, aesthetics, as well as logic, epistemology, and metaphysics. All proposals would be expected to apply philosophical rigour to the exploration of housing phenomena, whether this be the policy-making process, design, or the manner in which individuals and communities relate to housing. The series seeks an international and comparative focus and is particularly keen to include innovative and distinctly new approaches to the study of housing.

Please contact Peter King (pjking@dmu.ac.uk) with ideas for a book proposal or for further details.

Books in the series:

Thinking on Housing
Words, Memories, Use
Peter King

Social Justice in Contemporary Housing
Applying Rawls' Difference Principle
Helen Taylor

Place and Identity
Home as Performance
Joanna Richardson

Social Justice in Contemporary Housing

Applying Rawls' Difference Principle

Helen Taylor

Routledge
Taylor & Francis Group

LONDON AND NEW YORK

First published 2019 by Routledge

2 Park Square, Milton Park, Abingdon, Oxon OX14 4RN
605 Third Avenue, New York, NY 10017

Routledge is an imprint of the Taylor & Francis Group, an informa business

First issued in paperback 2021

Publisher's Note

The publisher has gone to great lengths to ensure the quality of this reprint but points out that some imperfections in the original copies may be apparent.

British Library Cataloguing-in-Publication Data
A catalogue record for this book is available from the British Library

Library of Congress Cataloging-in-Publication Data
A catalog record has been requested for this book

ISBN: 978-1-138-48607-2 (hbk)
ISBN: 978-1-03-217860-8 (pbk)
DOI: 10.1201/9781351046718

Typeset in Times New Roman
by codeMantra

Contents

Acknowledgements

Thank you to Chris and my parents for their unwavering support.

Introduction

This book is intended to appeal to readers both in academia engaged in discussions of philosophy, policy, or housing and practitioners in the housing sector. I hope it is appropriately balanced to do both.

There are some broad debates ongoing within academia on the bases and interaction of knowledge across different disciplinary areas. Does the abstract subject of philosophy have anything to say to political scientists studying policy? Should political scientists engage more deeply in philosophical concepts such as social justice that are used in political rhetoric? Is housing studies a discipline in and of itself, or is it a variety of other disciplines merely engaging in housing issues?

There are some serious debates going on between practitioners on the frontline of the housing sector. What is happening to cause increased poverty and homelessness and what can we do about it? What is the role of housing associations in tackling social problems? How do we understand our sector and our profession post Grenfell Tower?

I do not suggest for a minute that this book can answer these, but it will suggest a way that we can think harder about these frontline questions from within an academic discipline, which is understood to have issues of abstraction. Although engaged in robust philosophical theorising, the core argument within this text is that we should consider social policy from an account of what it enables people to do and be. The focus is on ensuring that individuals who are the least advantaged in society experience basic justice and are enabled through policy interventions to create an idea for the good life for themselves. This is nowhere more pertinent than within housing policy. From a practice perspective, the book provides a philosophical framework for us to explore issues such as the 'Bedroom Tax', increased rough sleeping, and benefit sanctions. From an academic perspective, the book contributes to two areas of debate regarding the pertinent use of philosophical concepts. I hope that it has something useful to say to both.

I argue in Chapter 1 that there is a correlation between the work of philosophers and policy-makers, and that the process of the creation of policy can be strengthened through the application of philosophy. This can be done through using philosophical concepts to analyse policy, as this book aims to do. Chapter 1 also goes on to assert that this application of philosophical analysis can be relevant in the case of housing policy in particular. I support the recent calls from Fitzpatrick and Watts (2018) for housing studies as a sub-discipline to engage in normative theorising, as well as analysing issues of housing through sociological or political theoretical frameworks. On this account, normative theory should be included more in the toolbox of theoretical frameworks drawn upon in order to analyse housing.

Moving onto the exposition and use of the work of John Rawls, I argue in Chapter 2 that not only can philosophical concepts be applied to housing issues but they *should* be. I provide the argument for normative engagement in policy based on the creation of legitimacy and propose that housing policy is a site of basic justice. Drawing on constructivist discussions around reasonableness, I outline that this form of normative analysis is engaged with in general terms both within a policy context and the context of everyday decision-making. The 'Bedroom Tax' is provided as an example here of an area of housing policy which can be seen as undermining the concept of reasonableness, and consequently basic justice.

Chapter 3 outlines in greater detail how Rawls' concept of justice as fairness, and in particular his tool of the difference principle, can be used as an analytical philosophical framework. The difference principle looks at the idea of equality and proposes that inequality in society is acceptable if the 'worst off' are made better off because of it. There are two key aspects to this tool; that it is created by and focusses on the least advantaged in society and that it dismisses the notion of retrogression of equality as being just. Chapter 4 highlights areas of contention with the Rawlsian account of justice, namely, its focus on primary goods as the metric of equality. It goes on to suggest a revised metric based on the capabilities approach and modifies aspects within the Rawlsian framework of justice to create viability in application of the principle as an everyday decision-making tool.

This approach of rebalancing aspects of the Rawlsian framework continues in Chapter 5, which provides an account of the concept of self-command within justice as fairness. This chapter draws on the work of Maslow (1943) and expands on the discussion of capabilities – what people are able to do and be. Here the core argument is made that policy relating to basic justice should enable individuals to have the social bases of effective agency – that individuals should be able to create a conception of the good life for themselves. The claim is made that there should be a scheme of redistribution within society, not so that specific goods are redistributed but so that individuals have the capacity to be able to decide what they should do and be. This idea of the ability to hold a conception of the good life is a core part of Rawls' account of human nature; if we are unable to exercise this, then our fundamental interests as human beings are being undermined.

Chapter 6 outlines how this modified difference principle looks and functions, pulling together the strands of theoretical development from the previous chapters. It states that the difference principle as a test for social justice in contemporary social policy asks the following two questions:

a   Does this policy enable the least advantaged individuals to be effective agents?
b   Does the policy make the least advantaged individuals in society worse off in terms of effective agency?

These two questions can be applied to social policies which relate to basic justice, as I suggest housing policies do. If the answers to both or either of these is no, then there is an issue with the policy in terms of both social justice and legitimacy. Chapter 6 demonstrates the new understandings of policy that can be developed through the use of this tool, looking at issues of homelessness and welfare reform.

The argument made throughout the book is that philosophical frameworks can usefully be applied to social policy, housing policy in particular, to give an account of social justice and legitimacy. The framework developed focusses on social justice in terms of what people are able to do and be and the role that institutions within the Rawlsian account of the basic structure have in enabling this. I hope it is a useful contribution both to thinking about the role of philosophy within the academy, but also within the practical policy sphere, to enable us to think differently about policy and questions of justice.

1   Housing studies, philosophy, and policy

This work focusses on the creation of a test for social justice that can be applied to social policy in general. In this work, however, I focus on how this can be developed in order to provide a critical understanding of issues related to housing. As well as contributing to debates around philosophy and policy, the book also therefore hopes to contribute to ongoing discussions within the sub-discipline of housing studies.

The epistemological foundations of housing studies

The idea of housing studies as a discipline in and of itself is contested. In 1992 Kemeny (p. 20) called for the housing studies community to develop an interest in the "fundamental prior questions concerning the grounds of knowledge of housing studies" and this discussion has continued. This section will outline contemporary discussions on the role and function of housing studies as an area of academic study. It will argue that there is merit in looking at housing issues and housing policy through a normative lens and that this approach broadens housing studies as a sub-discipline.

Housing studies as an area of academic enquiry is contested with debates around what 'counts' as part of the field, whether it is a discipline in its own right or a sub-discipline, and what theoretical frameworks are appropriate to apply to housing issues. Currently, there is no well-developed universal theory of housing on which to pin analytic inquiry. This therefore entails the application of other theoretical frameworks as the means by which to understand housing policy or issues. The discussion of whether there should be a universal theory of housing or which theoretical frameworks are appropriate for application to housing issues is ongoing. Allen (2009) has provided a framework to explore these discussions. He argues that little has changed in housing studies as a discipline since Kemeny's (1992) call to action. He notes that there has been a narrow interpretation of the call to bring theory back into the discipline, which has focussed on researchers applying theoretical frameworks from other disciplines to issues related to housing. There are simply two forms or approaches within the housing studies discipline according to Allen (2009). The first is empiricist housing studies; this is a distinctive activity which involves gathering knowledge about problems or concepts in an organised and systematic fashion. The second is theoretical housing studies; this involves providing depth and critical understanding to housing-related phenomena "which get beyond the naivety of empiricism" (2009, p. 54). Focussing on this second approach, Allen (2009, p. 54) claims:

> Housing researchers have narrowly interpreted Kemeny's (1992) call for a more theorized Housing Studies as an appeal for them to return to their own disciplines, and to 'bring back' theories of the state, ideology, power, and so on.

Kemeny (1992, pp. 3–4) discusses this approach within the broader epistemological framework of social science: "each discipline develops its own set of conceptual tools for the analysis of its particular dimension". Thus, sociology 'dimensions out' social relationships, economics does the same with the market, geography focusses on the dimension of space, and political science on the dimension of power and political institutions. Allen's (2009) critique is therefore that housing researchers do not have special insight into housing phenomena separate from the theoretical frameworks from other disciplines which they apply to this arena.

This discussion of the role of theory within housing studies leads to the further question of what the role of housing researchers is or should be. Should we be analysing housing phenomena according to theoretical frameworks of social relationships or market forces? Should we be searching for or creating a universal theory of housing with its own theoretical frameworks? Should we, as Allen (2009) would assert, give up the idea of housing studies as a discipline having any superior insight into housing issues? A further area of contention is the role that researchers do and should play in defining what constitutes a 'housing issue'. Kemeny (1992, pp. 20–21) asserts that housing researchers have "too easily accepted the way in which policy-makers define what is, or is not, a housing problem" and calls for researchers to take a more active role in defining housing issues informed by broader theoretical debates.

As with the idea of housing studies as a discipline in and of itself, the concept of a universal theory of housing has also been disputed. Linked to the discussion of 'dimensioning out', the consideration of the nature of housing as a subject raises questions of whether a holistic theoretical approach to housing phenomena can (and should) be developed. Ruonavaar (2018, p. 178) asserts "housing itself is not a research topic but a common denominator of a number of research topics" which includes "a multifaceted set of interconnected issues ranging from construction and supply, to wealth, financialization and asset-based welfare, to neighbourhood relations, to homelessness and acute disadvantage". Due to the wide range of phenomena that housing as an academic area of inquiry covers, it is not feasible to see this as a single unified research area but an amalgamation of a variety of different subject areas.

Fitzpatrick and Watts (2018) assert that instead of focussing on the development of a universal theory of housing, consideration should be given to the role of values in housing research. They call for more consideration to be given to normative issues within housing research, with a renewed theoretical engagement with questions of what 'ought' to be the case rather than a focus on what 'is' the case. They highlight the lack of this type of theoretical engagement with current issues which are addressed within housing research such as rights-based approaches to homelessness and social control measures related to redistribution. They go on to state (2018, p. 225):

> We would make a pitch for housing scholars to take much more seriously the contribution that could be made by political and moral philosophy in addressing these and other heavily normative questions…that abound in housing.

For Fitzpatrick and Watts (2018) one focus should be engaging with those 'ought' questions that arise in housing studies and are currently largely overlooked in terms of theoretical engagement. On their account, the theoretical frameworks or concepts of moral and political philosophy have a role to play in unpicking questions that are being asked by housing researchers to provide a normative analysis of current housing phenomena. They state (2018, p. 225):

> The careful attention to conceptual clarity, sound evidence, and logical reasoning found in the analytical philosophy tradition is … of fundamental and enduring importance to housing and social policy scholars who see to realize positive 'real world' impacts in line with their conception of justice.

Clapham (2018) notes that since Kemeny's critique, there has been a growing separation between housing researchers who focus on research with policy relevance and those who focus on theoretically informed research. The debate here, then, is not about the nature of the research being done but the purpose of the research; to inform and change policy or to develop theoretical insight. Clapham (2018) sets out a review of different types of policy processes and relates this to the type of research called on to evaluate these. He states (Clapham 2018, p. 173), "civil servants are supposed to read and commission 'neutral' and value free research to inform the policy-making process". Here the focus on 'good research' in the context of housing issues is research that is purely positivist and not theoretically informed. He (2018, p. 164) goes on to argue, however, that "theoretically oriented research can be policy relevant", and moreover (Clapham 2018, p. 176):

> Policy research needs to have an explicit theoretical foundation if it is able to explain phenomena and enable us to predict future issues and to guide the production of policy and to predict its impact.

For Clapham (2018), there should not be a division in housing research between that which is policy relevant and that which is theoretically informed.

As there is no universal theory of housing, the theoretical engagement with housing issues comes via frameworks from other fields. Although not necessarily problematic, he notes that this type of engagement is not always useful. He questions (2018, p. 176) whether there needs to be a theoretical framework which is unique to housing and concludes that "the most that can be expected is for the derivation of a number of trans-disciplinary concepts that could eventually be built into a theory of housing". There is therefore not a separation between theoretical and policy-oriented research, but a shift towards developing a universal theory of housing which can, and should, inform policy.

This book aims to engage with both Fitzpatrick and Watts' (2018) call for more philosophical engagement in housing and Clapham's (2018) argument around theoretically informed policy research. It will focus on the development of a normative theoretical approach to be used within housing studies, with a focus on questions of what 'ought' to be the case. Rather than giving an account of housing issues with reference to frameworks such as social relations or politics, it will focus on developing a standard of social justice which can be used to test the conceptualisation of social policy (including housing policy) and the subsequent responses to them. This work is firmly rooted within political philosophy with a focus on questions of justice. This framework will be applied to contemporary housing problems to provide different understandings of policy problems and develop answers to questions of what 'ought' to be the case.

The relationship between philosophy and policy

Before looking at whether philosophy can be successfully (and usefully) applied to housing policy, and social policy more generally, it is important to first briefly clarify both the role of policy in general terms, as well as the actors who are likely to be involved in the policy-making process. Philosophy can make a specific contribution to the concept of justification in policy-making, and it is the level of intervention linked to the implementation of social policy which creates this demand for justification.

When looking at what policy is, it is clear that it involves some form of intervention in individuals' lives. Dean (2012) outlines that the creation and introduction of social policy is a recognition of the interdependency upon each of the individuals living in a society. He states (2012, p. 6), "the social policies to which societies give birth may be understood as the way in which any particular society recognises and gives expression to the interdependency of its members". This builds on the work of Richard Titmuss (1955) who relates the development of social policy to the dependency of citizens on each other in order to meet needs. Discussing the creation of the welfare state, he outlines the recognition of these 'states of dependencies' as taking the form of collective responsibilities as fundamental to this. These 'states' take two forms; natural and manmade. Natural 'states of dependencies' include childhood, child bearing, and extreme old age. Manmade 'states' include those which are socially or culturally created such as situations of unemployment. These manmade 'states' involve some form of curtailment of earning power, such that an individual cannot meet their own needs. All individuals will experience some form of dependency – either natural or manmade – over their life course. The existence of social policy, therefore, is the recognition of both of these dependencies experienced by individuals and of a collective responsibility for these states. Social policy, therefore, intervenes in individuals' lives at these times to provide either a remedy or mitigation for the type of 'state of dependency' which is being experienced.

There is, then, a link between the existence of policy and a form of intervention in individuals' lives. It is this link that enables the case to be made for the potential inclusion of philosophy within the policy-making process. I argue that it is the very nature of this inextricable link between policy and intervention that demands the provision of justification for policy. Underpinning this book as a whole is the argument that due to the nature of social policy as a form of intervention, a normative element has been built into the process. This normative element places a duty for a requirement of justification onto the policy-making process, which I will go on to argue in Chapter 2 can be provided through a consideration of the concept of reasonableness.

We can further add weight to this claim that justification is required due to the level of intervention social policy entails by looking at the question of what policy is and how it is made. Hall (1993) discusses policy creation as a form of social learning which can conclude with a paradigm shift in approach. He draws on the work of Heclo (1974) outlining (Hall 1993, pp. 305–6) that "policy-making is a form of collective puzzlement on society's behalf". Although Hall goes on to criticise the narrow focus of this approach, it is an interesting position to consider when looking at the role of policy and questioning whether philosophy can have a part in this process. If policy-making is the process by which the state interprets, and then creates, a response to issues experienced by citizens, then philosophers, in their role of taking a systematic approach to difficult questions, should be involved. Within the policy-making process decisions are made regarding the nature of an issue that is to be addressed, how this is understood as a policy problem, and what the solution to this problem should be. Defining terms and analysing sequential arguments occurs, therefore, within each discipline. This further supports the argument for justification: if policy-makers are acting as the collective decision-makers on behalf of citizens, there needs to be a form of accountability for the decisions made in this process.

Fischer (2000) discusses the issue of the relationship between the use of experts in policy development and citizen participation in more detail. He builds on concerns from Dewey (1927) that the increasing complexity of modern, technological society undermines the space for citizens to be involved in deliberation of and decision-making within a democracy. Fischer (2000, p. 2) argues that "citizen participation contributes normatively to the legitimacy of policy development and implementation". There has been a shift, first recognised in Dewey's work in the 1920s, towards looking to knowledge experts to make political decisions about policy. Fischer (2000, p. 1) characterises this challenge: "are not the knowledge elites more likely to support the values of both social justice and efficiency" in decision-making? The conflict, then, lies between the fundamental role of the citizen within a society functioning as a democracy and the capacity of citizens to adequately contribute to decision-making that regards complex issues. This shift towards experts and away from citizens therefore has an impact on normative justification. Fischer (2000, p. 7) states:

> The increasing complexity of social problems, giving rise to increasing specialisation and the expansion of elite 'public policy specialists' puts the Western polyarchies in the position of being replaced by a 'quasi-guardianship' of autonomous experts, no longer accountable to the ordinary public.

Fischer (2000, p. 8) goes on to outline further issues with this reliance on experts: that, in fact, it has been seen that experts are also unable to engage with these complex problems. Also, that expertise "turns out not to be the neutral objective phenomenon that it has purported to be". Often, expertise has been found to be influenced by ideological motives, undermining the justification of reliance on experts because of their supposed objective knowledge. This conflict between the role of experts and citizens is often based on assumptions about the cognitive ability of citizens. Experts are seen to be more appropriate decisions-makers because of their capacity to engage with complex issues in a robust and rigorous way. Experts need to be able to understand and present solutions to complicated issues, as well as understand how this relates to citizens' views on the issue. Fischer (2000, p. 9) states that experts need to be able to present an "understanding [of] how different citizens arrive at their own judgements of such issues". The inclusion of philosophers or use of philosophy within policy-making decisions can be seen to go some way to address this conflict. When looking at the role of expertise, philosophers can provide a way of engaging with, and advising on, normative judgement and the inclusion of multiple groups within decision-making, as well as giving an account of the development of judgements. My theoretical framework will go on to outline a way in which citizens using ordinary decision-making procedures can be part of a process which provides normative justification for policy decisions.

The very nature of policy consists of a normative element around the interventionist nature of the impact of policy on people. Indeed, Hall (1993, p. 292) states, "policy-making in virtually all fields takes place within the context of a particular set of ideas that recognise some ... as more legitimate than others". To ensure that the interests of the decision-makers match the interests of citizens, it is crucial that a form of scrutiny takes place. I argue that philosophers are well placed to undertake this critical approach in order to discover justification for policy that is being made. In the context of housing policy, this point has already been highlighted by Fitzpatrick and Watts (2018): housing researchers should be concerned with the 'ought' questions underpinned by moral and political philosophical concepts.

It is not the case that justification on normative grounds is not already sought as part of the policy-making process. Particular mechanisms are also used to provide a form of justification for the impact of policies. For example, Equality Impact Assessments (EIAs) are a tool by which policy can be analysed to understand the impact on individuals who fall into categories with protected characteristics in the 2010 Equality Act (Equality and Human Rights Commission, 2017). Individuals who receive negative treatment due to particular characteristics such as disability, age, or religion have been subject to an illegal act. This is an assessment which can be applied to policy and the behaviour of public bodies in order to protect those who are defined as particularly vulnerable. Their existence embodies a normative claim; the concept of equality is valued and a particular range of individuals should be treated in a particular way. However, this claim focusses on a specific set of individuals and a specific value that is to be upheld.

Rather than a descriptive account of the relationship between policy and people, my test for social policy takes a normative position (broadening the approach to EIAs), arguing that, due to the intervention of the state in individuals' lives through the mechanism of social policy, a form of justification should be provided. In this work, I use housing as an example of policy which can be subject to this form of normative justificatory process. However, the test could be used across social policy in order to give an account of legitimacy and basic justice.

Applied philosophy

I have outlined so far that there is a normative element to all policy which requires justification with regard to the intervention in individuals' lives. Again, as with the relationship between policy and justification, this is not a new concept. A number of philosophers undertake the broad project of applied philosophy, which brings together philosophical theoretical frameworks with particular issues or experiences within society. This can be issue-focussed such as looking at the relationship between conceptions of political obligation and specific prison systems, for example (Holroyd, 2010). However, this can also be methodological such as the engagement of philosophers with policy development more broadly. The basis of my research is the argument that social policy is a suitable area in which Rawlsian concepts of justice can be applied. As with the general application of philosophy to policy, Rawlsian theorists have generally looked at the application of justice as fairness to health (Daniels, 1985) or global justice policy contexts (Pogge, 2004) but not to more domestic areas such as housing policy. There are, therefore, two spaces that this project aims to contribute to: first, the minimal engagement of philosophy with public policy and second, when philosophers do engage with practical issues, which is likely to be in the area of health and other distributive goods – rarely housing (King, 2011). We can see this as an echo of Clapham's (2018) dichotomy of the use of theory in housing, either used to further develop theory or as a means to better analyse policy. I hope for this project to add to the emerging field of the application of philosophy to public policy and be persuasive in the argument that housing is an important area for normative justification to be sought.

The first approach to engaging philosophy with policy can be seen as taking theory to practice, or 'dimensioning out' philosophical concepts to echo Kemeny (1992). Peter King (2011) addresses a number of the issues outlined earlier in a paper on the use of a 'toolkit approach' to applying political philosophy to policy (housing policy in particular). He states that the paper emerged as an attempt to answer a number of questions. The first is the question that is often asked of this type of work, which is (2011, p. 110) "what has this got to do with real world housing problems?" The second regards why theorists tend to ignore housing as a policy area by which to explore their application of philosophy. Addressing the first question, King outlines (2011, p. 110) that his work in this piece has a "metatheoretical" purpose; he wants to explore how far theorists such as Nozick (1974) can be used within a policy context. He emphasises that his work is a response to the ongoing conflict between theory and practice, where (2011, p. 109) "the discussion of theory...is a luxury or indulgence that should not be undertaken whilst serious issues...exist". He cites (2011, p. 109) similar concerns from Bo Bengtsson (2001) on this issue: "political philosophies seldom discuss housing, whereas government papers on housing seldom discuss political philosophy". King argues that taking a 'toolkit approach' to the theories of major thinkers would combat this divide and provide a useful contribution to the policy literature.

Regarding the second question King, again, draws on Bengtsson and highlights (2011, p. 111) that thinkers such as Rawls, Dworkin, and Sen all touch on issues relating to primary goods, resources, and capabilities yet "none of these three writers explicitly discuss housing, not even as an illustration". King goes on to explain why this might be the case, and why other policy areas such as health are preferable for this type of application of theory to practice. First, he highlights that housing is less epistemologically complex than other goods. People understand housing and housing need, and this type of good is more amenable to choice. Determining housing need is therefore (2011, p. 112) "less opaque" than understanding need in other policy areas, and the need for housing is indeed a permanent condition rather than a flexible condition such as health. Second, King outlines that housing is an essentially practical activity and can be seen to require less reflection for decisions to be made as they can be understood in terms of programmatic standards. He states (2011, p. 112), "the nature of the ethical and technical dilemmas in housing is not the same level of complexity and controversy that one finds in healthcare". This can be linked to the type of intervention required to provide each type of good. For health, the nature of the state's intervention is reactive; healthcare is needed only when something has gone wrong. With housing, however, the need relating to the good is different. Government is, typically, always generically involved in the provision of housing in regard to issues such as standards, the availability of land, and where housing can be built. This is more of a proactive involvement than often seen with issues such as healthcare. Finally, King emphasises that the nature of housing is more culturally determined than other goods such as healthcare, and therefore we could be less able to make universal statements about housing unless in a general sense.

King asserts that by using the application of philosophical concepts to specific housing policy issues we can reverse the questions highlighted earlier to be able to have a critical tool which asks (2011, p. 113), "what use is (this form of) housing to us?" He goes on to outline a number of potential issues with this form of methodology, namely, that there is a variance in the approaches taken by philosophers and policy-makers in terms of decision-making. King highlights that policy-makers are not able to take the tabula rasa approach as often found with philosophical frameworks and instead have to work with conditions and situations that are already in place. He notes (2011, p. 118), "the problem therefore is how we match up an abstract, if internally consistent, argument to a changing policy environment". King also notes (2011, p. 118) that the use of these philosophical frameworks will not deliver "hard and fast policy solutions" but an ideal type of argument by which specific policy can be measured. It is the nature of this ideal standard which I will be using to formulate my test.

King argues that the 'toolkit approach' proposed by Foucault (1994) can be used to match up the theoretical approaches of political philosophy within the dynamic policy sphere. Foucault suggests that his political work can be understood as a toolkit from which others can draw in order to apply abstract philosophy to particular policy areas. He states (1994, p. 523), "I would like my books to be a kind of toolbox which others can rummage through to find a tool which they can use however they wish in their own area". On this account, there are a number of devices and mechanisms within theories that can be chosen to be applied to policy issues depending on the context and content of the policy. In his own work, King uses Robert Nozick's (1974) theory of private property to analyse the topic of housing and, more specifically, looks at the concept of side constraint as the basis of a phenomenological study of the use of private housing. He states (2011, p. 119), "we might not wish to achieve Nozick's utopia, but like all abstract principles, it forms a model through which to assess the direction of policy".

King asserts, therefore, that theoretical frameworks provided by thinkers such as Nozick can be used to critically analyse contemporary policy and outlines three ways in which this can happen. First, these grand concepts can be used to assess existing and past policies against clear normative principles. He gives the example of devices within both Nozick's and Rawls' theories of justice as setting specific standards by which to measure or test policy. These devices can offer (2011, p. 118) "some sort of absolute standard or pole by which we can determine both the nature and direction of the policy". King emphasises that Rawls' difference principle is one such device, and this is how I intend to use my modified account of the principle. Second, King outlines that the ideas can also offer the basis by which new policies and commitments can be developed with a (2011, p. 119) "principled underpinning". Again, we can see how theoretical frameworks can set clear normative standards by which policy – either established or emerging – can be scrutinised. Finally (2011, p. 119), "we can use grand theory to establish clear distinctions between policies through looking at their normative underpinnings". A comparative approach can be taken to policies, again based on a normative theoretical backdrop. King states (2011, p. 120) that these critical approaches to policy can be taken by extending these devices from within theoretical frameworks beyond the "specific theoretical context" in which they are written and applying them to new situations. Importantly, he argues (2011, p. 120) that this can be done "in a way that is consistent with...[the] construction of these devices and mechanisms".

Presenting this approach, King emphasises (2011, p. 120) the necessity of applied philosophers to "think clearly of the context for our argument and so which elements of a thinker's position we can use to assist us". By taking a 'toolkit approach' we have a range of theoretical devices and mechanisms available to us to apply to policy, but we need to be sure that these have both utility and relevance. King states:

> We should recognise that there is a huge library of works which offer the opportunity to develop our understanding of housing policy and its connection with the normative principles we use to justify our place in the world.
>
> (2011, p. 121)

Jonathan Wolff has written on his broad experience of being engaged in public policy development as a philosopher, asserting (2011, p. 1) that "political philosophers have a responsibility to take matters of public policy seriously". He has been involved in a range of projects of this nature, from being commissioned by the Liquor, Gambling, and Data Protection Unit to be involved in a review of gambling law, to involvement in the Nuffield Council on Bioethics Working Party looking at the ethics of scientific experiments on animals. He outlines his starting assumption for this type of work as:

> Moral and political philosophy…is made for the analysis of public policy, exploring foundational values and consolidating them into theories and prototype polices that could…fit practical needs to improve the moral quality of our public lives.
>
> (2011, pp. 2–3)

Here we can see how his work fits with King's; both are arguing for the application of philosophy to questions of policy in order to provide a normative test or underpinning for decision-making. Although committed to the use of political philosophy in public policy, Wolff also notes that there are competing objectives and processes within the different spheres. In one discipline, disagreement is encouraged and discussion enabled. In another, the ultimate aim is to provide practical solutions to pressing issues. Again, this can be seen to relate back to King's discussion of the conflict between theory and practice. In philosophy we can indulge in discussion around specific details of what can be seen as abstract concepts in order to achieve internal validity. Within the policy discipline practical solutions are demanded, normally within a reactive context. We can see how the rhetoric around not having the space to engage with theory, when there are pressing matters of public concern to be addressed, can develop.

The second model by which philosophy can engage with policy, then, can be explained as from practice to theory. Wolff goes on to highlight three further key areas in which the policy arena debate differs from philosophical argument. First, he asserts that there is little space for 'agreeing to disagree' (as is often the case with philosophy) as practical solutions are needed. The aim of the project is different; in philosophy we are aiming for an internally valid, robust, argument. In policy, we are aiming for a pragmatic and practical solution to a specific and, perhaps, urgent issue which can gain general consensus from decision-makers. Second, within public policy there is an inevitable bias towards the status quo which can be obstructive to developing new normative thinking. As highlighted by King, there is rarely a tabula rasa for policy-makers. The context in which decisions are made are constrained by pre-existing standards and conditions. Third, in developing policy, whether a moral view is correct takes second place to whether it is widely shared or accepted. Again, the emphasis here is on consensus rather than internal validity. In the next chapter, I will go on to address this issue in terms of the existence of 'reasonableness' between individuals and the contribution of this towards a political concept of legitimacy. Wolff states, however, that rather than dismissing philosophical engagement due to these conflicts in aims, academics should explore how to connect philosophical reasoning with public policy and foster this public acceptance. He comments (2011, p. 203), "what matters in public policy debate is not convincing yourself that you have the right position but carrying others with you".

Explaining his methodological approach to this form of engagement, Wolff notes that the project of connecting philosophy with public policy must engage in 'bottom-up theorising'. He states that there are two initial approaches to this: first, trying to understand enough about the policy area under examination and the moral difficulties that arise here and second, to connect these difficulties or dilemmas with patterns of philosophical reflection. As previously noted, this could be achieved through undertaking a 'toolkit approach', where there is a careful consideration and application of philosophical devices or mechanisms to specific policy issues. From his experience of this type of theorising, Wolff has identified an alternative methodology by which to undertake this type of analysis. This methodology forms a four-part process. The first step is to fully investigate current practice; second, current regulations and the legislative processes by which the legislation is formed need to be understood; and third, a history of how these processes played out in regard to the specific policy area needs to be constructed. These first three processes can be seen as part of an attempt to understand the pre-existing conditions that are already in place around a policy area. Finally, there needs to be a level of understanding of what people currently agree or disagree about in relation to the policy area. Again, this links back to the potential difference around philosophy and policy in terms of consensus and internal validity. Wolf (2011, p. 192) asserts, "philosophers sometimes fall short of taking up the challenge of thinking hard about question of the process, and even more importantly, consequences of implementation".

We can see from King and Wolff that there are value-based arguments for the application of philosophy to policy. Both highlight similar conflicts between the nature of the disciplines involved, with emphasis being placed on understanding challenges that might already be in place and developing a consensus on proposed changes or decisions. I also argue that there is a normative imperative for philosophers to engage with public policy in order to provide the level of scrutiny that has been outlined by both Wolff and King. By doing so, we are able to use 'grand concepts' to scrutinise political decision-making and to provide normative theoretical frameworks to be used to test current – or support developing – policy.

Policy: homelessness and housing first

Jeremy Waldron (1991) provides an example of a 'top-down' exposition of a concrete policy issue through a broad conceptual framework. Rather than presenting a methodological account of how philosophy might engage with policy, he uses the framework of freedom rights to explore the issue of homelessness. We can see in his work, then, a specific example of how normative concepts can create new understanding of housing-related issues and the contribution that the application of philosophical frameworks can make to conceptualising policy issues.

Waldron asserts (1991, p. 296), "homelessness is a matter of the utmost concern in relation to some of the most fundamental and abstract principles of liberal value". He comments that the recognition of this is lacking amongst theorists, who acknowledge issues such as torture as a key liberal concern but do not often consider issues of housing. Responding to this, he creates a theory of homelessness as an issue of social freedom to show that using an abstract philosophical framework can help understand current housing policy issues and inform responses to these questions. Waldron asserts (1991, p. 296), "everything that is done has to be done somewhere...no one is free to perform an action unless there is somewhere he is free to perform it". He then goes on to outline the connection between freedom, action, and the impact of property rights on this.

Noting that there are three types of property rights – private, collective, and common – he asserts that different rights to property have differing impacts on individuals' abilities to have space in which to act. The ability to act in an area under private ownership is clearly defined to the owners of that space or property. Access to collective property is usually determined by officials acting as representatives of the community, and they define who can act in that space. Common property is a sub-class of collective property, but one which is fairly easy for anyone to access. Waldron highlights (1991, p. 299) that for an individual who is homeless "there is no place governed by a private property rule where he is allowed to be". He further notes the increasing regulation of public property such as streets and parks where, although access is allowed, some actions are prohibited within those spaces. Waldron asserts that this can be justified through the complementarity of accessing both public and private space – some activities are only to be undertaken within a private space, and these are inappropriate in a public space. This complementarity, however, breaks down for those who have no access to private space. He comments (1991, p. 301), "what is emerging...is a state of affairs in which...citizens have no place to perform elementary human activities like urinating, washing, sleeping, cooking, eating, and standing around".

This lack of ability to undertake core human functions creates the basis for Waldron's theory of homelessness as an issue of freedom. He argues (1991, p. 302), "all actions involve a spatial component"; therefore, if an individual does not have a space to undertake a certain action, they are not free to do it. Without the space to fulfil basic human functions such as washing and sleeping a homeless individual is (1991, p. 302) "comprehensively unfree" and therefore he concludes (1991, p. 306), "homelessness consists in unfreedom". He notes (1991, p. 320) that the actions that are restricted for a person experiencing homelessness are "basic to the sustenance of a decent or healthy life, in some cases basic to the sustenance of life itself" and often function as the preconditions for other activities. He states that it is degrading and undignified for actions that are (1991, p. 320) "both urgent and quotidian" to be denied, and broader social and economic opportunities rely on the fulfilling of these functions. Individuals' agency is therefore undermined through the condition of homelessness as the most basic freedoms are undermined.

By applying a theory of freedom to the policy matter of homelessness, Waldron has created an approach to homelessness, which regards it as a matter of freedom and therefore agency. He comments (1991, p. 324), "perhaps the strongest argument for thinking about homelessness as an issue of freedom is that it forces us to see people in need as agents". By approaching the issue from a broad philosophical framework, Waldron has revised the understanding of the concept of homelessness, which could lead to alternative policy responses. The analysis of this specific housing issue has not focussed on social relations or empirical inquiry but looked at how the moral concept of freedom can be used to unpick a complex and immediate housing problem.

King builds on this theory of housing as a freedom right and argues (2003, p. 661) that "one can build from a common sense perception of necessary human functionings to a conception of the right to housing as an elemental condition for human flourishing". He states that understanding the issue of housing in the context of freedom rights can have five broad impacts on everyday policy-making. First, it provides a generally applicable argument for housing, which is cross-culture and cross-tenure. Second, it places housing alongside other welfare goods. Instead of emphasising the distinct needs of the minority of the population who need urgent housing support, which can lead to entrenched social exclusion, it concentrates on the common, and universal, features of rights. Third, the argument places access to housing as a right alongside property rights – again, not distinguishing between tenures. Fourth, it gives weight to choice-based approaches to housing. Finally, it rejects discussions of resources available and political priorities to recognise the moral imperative within housing as a freedom right. He concludes (2003, p. 671), "this rights-based argument can be used to claim that housing is an elemental right upon which other basic human functions depend". This understanding of homelessness and housing might have an impact on considerations around intentionality and priority need testing to qualify for a duty for housing, or for such schemes such as the Right to Buy. By understanding the need in a different way, as well as the impact of the lack of provision of housing, policy could be formulated according to different priorities.

We can use Waldron's model of an understanding of homelessness as an issue of social freedom to explore the specific policy example of Housing First. This model of service provision started in New York in 1992 and has developed across the US. It is now gaining traction in the UK, with a commitment from the Welsh Government to implement this within housing policy in Wales. The underlying tenets of the model are as follows:

- Individuals are given immediate housing without any requirement to prove that they can successfully live independently
- There is the provision of floating support delivered to individuals in their own homes
- Housing is regarded as a basic human right
- Respect, warmth, and compassion should be given to each client
- The organisation providing the housing commits to working with the individual for as long as they need
- Accommodation is scattered so as to provide integration with the wider community, and this accommodation is normally from the Private Rented Sector
- There is a separation of housing and services; clients' engagement with one does not affect the provision of the other
- Consumer choice and self-determination are supported
- A harm reduction approach is taken in regard to drug and alcohol consumption

(Bretherton and Pleace, 2015)

The traditional model of support for individuals with complex needs is based on housing readiness and focusses on a staircase approach to accessing permanent accommodation. These steps involve an initial contact with outreach workers or a day centre, then a space in a direct access hostel, followed by time in a specialist hostel, before the individual is able to access either semi-independent or shared accommodation, and then finally an independent tenancy (Shelter England, 2008). Progression along this staircase is dependent on individuals appropriately engaging with the support provided and demonstrating that they have made progression with their complex needs, such as substance misuse or mental health, thus proving that they are 'housing ready'.

Housing First as an approach rejects the idea of individuals proving that they are 'housing ready' and instead provides a permanent tenancy with client-centred floating support to be delivered at home. These tenancies are usually scatter-site housing within ordinary neighbourhoods and communities. Sarah Johnsen (2018) offers four reasons why Housing First as a model of service provision has been successful. First, she highlights longevity; that individuals are given secure housing and support that does not ask for them to prove that they are 'housing ready'. This dispels anxiety around 'what happens next' in their housing journey and enables them to focus on support. Johnsen states, "it is hard to overstate how significant this can be in facilitating recovery". The second area she highlights is that of flexibility of support. The nature of the provision within a Housing First model allows for "peaks and troughs" of engagement which engenders a positive relationship between users and service providers. Johnsen states Housing First models support a "truly client-centred approach respects individual choice and gives a greater sense of control over their [service users'] lives". The third area of success is the "stickability" of Housing First services. Johnsen outlines that many service users have been excluded from mainstream services as they failed to engage on the terms set, leaving individuals feeling like they have been rejected and are unworthy of help. Housing First enables an honest conversation to be had between individuals and support workers as their housing situation is not subject to engagement or 'success'. Finally, Housing First accommodation is normal accommodation. Tenancies are offered within communities and neighbourhoods and support is delivered within individuals' home. Johnsen asserts, "Housing First also offers what many perceive as an invaluable 'escape' from potentially destructive cultures on the street and in congregate forms of accommodation".

Housing First as a solution to homelessness provides us with an insight to the characterisation of homelessness as an issue in the first place, and we can see that this broad approach can be seen to fit Waldron's theory of social freedoms. Housing is regarded as a right, which all individuals should have access to. The model provides private space as the first element of its support system. Individuals do not have to prove that they are able to live independently but accommodation is initially provided for them, with support to follow. We can see, therefore, that a characterisation of the problem of homelessness is focussed on the lack of private space for those who are homeless. The Housing First model provides this private space as the first step of the process, with broader (and softer) support services being put in place to enable the individual to successfully live in that accommodation.

The idea of individuals within society being free and equal, and therefore having the right to the capacity for effective agency, is crucial within Waldron's theory and is something I will return to when discussing my metric for the test. It is important to recognise the importance of Waldron's theory as a contribution to a different understanding of homelessness, wherein the physical space that you are able to access as an individual impacts on your ability to act as an effective agent. The application of Waldron's model, therefore, shows us the utility of applying normative concepts to specific policy areas. The model developed a broad normative concept – social freedom – into a framework used to analyse the issue of homelessness. This was then applied to more tangible policy development of Housing First approaches to service provision. By applying this framework and set of concepts, we developed a different understanding of both the issue of homelessness and subsequently an appropriate policy response.

This chapter has explored the relationship between philosophy and policy, and the way in which we can create new understandings of policy issues through applying theoretical frameworks. The application of normative theory to tangible policy questions has been explored and we have seen an initial example of this through the application of Waldron's theoretical approach to Housing First as a type of service delivery. The subsequent chapters focus on the philosophical underpinnings for this relationship between philosophy and policy before developing the particular way that this can happen through a revised difference principle.

2   The role of the reasonable in public justification

Introduction

Shaun Young states, "the notion of 'reason(ableness)' has been a central feature of liberalism since [it] first emerged as a coherent philosophical project" (2008, p. 257). In this chapter I will be outlining accounts of reasonableness from John Rawls and Thomas Scanlon and discussing how this can be used in my project of creating a test for social justice in contemporary social policy. I will begin by outlining the approaches both theorists take to this concept and go on to describe how the concept can be understood to have a regulatory function. In the last section of the chapter, I will argue that the idea of reasonableness should be extended beyond individual decision-making to be used in a structural context based on an account of political legitimacy. It is this structural aspect, based on reciprocity between individuals in the scheme of social cooperation, which enables boundaries to be set on individual action. This theoretical framework will set the scene for me to build the argument for a difference principle to be applied to social policy.

The two moral powers

Both Scanlon and Rawls provide accounts of motivation as an alternative to utilitarianism. Instead of motivation being based on the measure of the greatest pleasure or well-being for individuals, they broadly base motivation on the justification of actions as reasonable to others, who are interested in the concept of justification. A fundamental difference therefore between the two types of account is their relationship to the notion of public justification. On a utilitarian account, there is no requirement for justification to be public but simply justifiable according to consequentialist logic. The liberal accounts characterised by Scanlon and Rawls, however, place the commitment to public justification at the core. Although Scanlon's project is one of moral constructivism whilst Rawls is looking for a political account of motivation, it is useful to look at both accounts of reasonableness within these contexts. I will outline Scanlon's account in a subsequent paragraph; here I will address Rawls' approach to fair terms reasonableness from within *Political Liberalism*.

In *Political Liberalism*, Rawls addresses the question "how is it possible for there to exist over time a just and stable society of free and equal citizens who still remain profoundly divided by reasonable religious, philosophical, and moral doctrines?" (1996, p. 47). He argues that a political conception of justice can be applied in this context which will lead to an overlapping consensus of reasonable comprehensive doctrines affirmed by almost all citizens. This political conception needs to be shared by all citizens to be able to create the basis of public reason regarding political questions of both constitutional essentials and basic justice. It is this focus on a shared political conception of justice which leads to the introduction of the concept of 'reasonable' as the basis on which individuals can agree about political issues regardless of whether their comprehensive moral doctrines differ.

Rawls states that there are two moral powers within his conception of the person; the capacity to be reasonable and the capacity to be rational, which individuals need to be able to exercise to a minimum level to be considered to be free and equal citizens. The exercise of these two powers is the basis of equal democratic citizenship. Rawls characterises this as a quotidian distinction that individuals understand, and states, "in everyday speech we are aware of a difference and common examples readily bring it out" (1996, p. 48). This is an important aspect to his account from the context of reasonableness operating within a scheme of social cooperation among free, equal, and disinterested individuals. He outlines that to be rational is to be able to hold a conception of the good and to be able to "form, to revise, and rationally to pursue a conception of one's rational advantage, or good" (1985, p. 233). This idea is distinct from the moral power of reasonableness and applies to a single, unified agent such as an individual or a corporate person. He states that this power entails the agent seeking ends or interests that are their own and deciding the means by which to pursue these aims. The agents are not being entirely self-interested, however, and do have the capacity for affections and attachments to others within the concept of developing and pursuing their own ends and conceptions of the good.

The capacity of reasonableness is "public in a way that the rational is not" (Rawls 1996, p. 53). To be reasonable is to understand that others also have a motivation to pursue their own conceptions of the good and to act in way which recognises this. For Rawls, this moral power is one that enables individuals to "enter as equals the public world of others" (1996, p. 53). Here, the focus is on recognising the role of others within a scheme of cooperation through reciprocity; other individuals also have their conceptions of the good which they wish to pursue. As all individuals are free and equal within the scheme, reasonableness ensures reciprocal relationships so that all have the freedom by which to pursue their conceptions of the good. Reasonable individuals, therefore, are aware that limits might have to be put on their own actions due to their membership of a social scheme of cooperation comprised of free and equal individuals. Rawls states, "reasonable persons...are not moved by the general good as such but desire for its own sake a social world in which they, as free and equal, can cooperate with others on terms, all can accept" (1996, p. 50). Rawls goes on to state that "as reasonable [people] we must assess the strength of people's claims, not only against our claims but...on our common practices or institutions" (1996, p. 56).

Regarding the relationship between the two moral powers, Rawls outlines that these are two distinct, independent, ideas which are complementary rather than derivative. These powers work together to enable individuals to have both the capacity for a conception of the good and the capacity for a sense of justice. He states:

> They work in tandem to specify the idea of fair terms of cooperation, taking into account the kind of social cooperation in question, the nature of the parties and their standing with respect to one another.
>
> (1996, p. 52)

The term reasonable can be seen from the beginning then to be fixed to the concept of individuals living together in a scheme of social cooperation. Through exercising these two moral powers "in tandem" (1985, p. 52) individuals have to acknowledge that they have interests that they want to pursue, but also recognise the constraint that others' reasonable conceptions of the good place on their actions. Rawls states, "reasonable persons...are not moved by the general good as such but desire for its own sake a social world in which they, as free and equal, can cooperate with others on terms all can accept" (1996, p. 50).

It is this emphasis on the public that separates reasonableness from rationality.

It is the first aspect of Rawls' account of reasonableness: fair terms reasonableness, which I want to focus on as the basis for argument on political legitimacy. This asserts that individuals must have a willingness to propose and honour fair terms of cooperation. Rawls states:

> Persons are reasonable in one basic aspect when...they are ready to propose principles and standards as fair terms of cooperation and to abide by them willingly, given the assurance that others will do likewise.
>
> (1996, p. 49)

It is this aspect of Rawls' work which most readily emphasises the social nature of the capacity for reasonableness and distinguishes it from the moral power of rationality. On this account, for individuals to be reasonable, they have to be able to understand their place within a scheme of social cooperation and revise or limit their actions accordingly. They must be able to propose principles and standards which would constitute fair terms for the other members of the scheme to accept, and they must also recognise the requirement to willingly abide by other principles and standards that have been proposed and accepted as fair terms. Rawls comments, "these terms...specify the reasons we are to share and publicly recognise before one another as grounding our social relations" (1996, p. 53). It is this interrelation with others within the scheme of social cooperation and the role of fair terms reasonableness within this which enables individuals to "work out the framework for the public social world" (1996, p. 53).

It is the moral power of reasonableness, working in tandem with the moral power of rationality, which outlines how individuals can reach agreements as reasonable members of a scheme of social cooperation. This in turn, outlines the framework by which individuals within the scheme may operate. Rawls states, "in a reasonable society...all have their own rational ends they hope to advance, and all stand ready to propose fair terms that others may reasonably be expected to accept" (1996, p. 54) given their differing ends. It is important to note again, that Rawls understands this distinction between reasonable and rational as one which individuals recognise and accept within everyday decision-making. We can see this in our own quotidian understanding of the difference between reasonable and rational in everyday decision-making. For example, we understand that it might be rational for an umpire who is affiliated with a certain cricket team to adjust their judgements in order to favour their team. We also understand that this would not be reasonable and would undermine the fairness of the game. It would be in my own interest to get a seat on a coach for a long journey, but it would not be reasonable to push all the passengers in front of me in the queue out of the way so I could do so. The account that Rawls provides a scheme of cooperation comprised of reasonable individuals should not be an abstract theoretical position but a reflection of how a real society can and should operate. Rawls states

> this reasonable society is neither a society of saints nor a society of the self-centred. It is very much a part of our ordinary human world, not a world we think of much virtue, until we find ourselves without it.
>
> (1996, p. 54)

As highlighted, Thomas Scanlon (2000) provides a similar account of reasonableness to Rawls based on justifying decisions to individuals with social schemes as an alternative to a utilitarian account. The important aspect of this account is the configuration of the test for reasonableness. A key function of Scanlon's account, which sits in comparison to Rawls', is his emphasis on the rejectability of an action based on reasonableness. On this account "it is the reasonableness of rejecting a principle, rather than the reasonableness of accepting it, on which the moral argument turns" (2000, p. 598). To provide further argument for this, Scanlon gives the example of a group of self-sacrificing individuals who are also the 'worst off' in society. He outlines that this group of people could easily accept a principle or decision which could be described as unreasonable but would not be judged as such on an account that focusses on a positive approach to reasonableness. This case would not occur with the focus on whether actions or principles can be reasonably rejected, rather than accepted. Scanlon asserts, "the source of motivation that is directly triggered by the belief that an action is wrong is the desire to be able to justify one's actions to others on grounds that they could not reasonably reject" (p. 600). Moral justification on this account is therefore sought through the approval of others within the scheme of who could accept or reject an action. Rightness is that which cannot be reasonably rejected by others, wrongness that which could be rejected. Scanlon's test, therefore, is that of reasonable rejectability. Principles and actions are either permitted or wrong based on whether they can be reasonably rejected by others within the social scheme. If there is no reasonable rejection of a principle, then it is morally acceptable. Principles can be reasonably rejected when individuals are burdened to an extent whereby their agency is undermined.

The use of reasonableness as a regulatory mechanism

Both Rawls' and Scanlon's accounts can be seen to use the concept of 'reasonable' within a regulatory context. For Rawls, his conception of the person includes the conception of 'reasonable' as the complementary moral power to rationality. This power can be seen as regulating the potential actions that individuals take based on their desire to pursue their conceptions of the good. As emphasised earlier, the capacity to be reasonable is intrinsically linked with the social aspect of individuals within a scheme of cooperation and can be understood to be the basis of the framework for the social public world. In Scanlon's account, individuals' desires for action are regulated by the test of whether the principles or actions that follow from them can be reasonably rejected by others. As noted, this regulative function is also a direct result of individuals acting within a scheme of social cooperation which incorporates other reasonable beings with first order desires.

Margaret Moore (1996) more strongly makes the case for the concept of reasonableness to have a regulatory function. Highlighting the relationship between justice as prior to the good in a liberal polity, Moore asserts, "at the level of the person, individual actions, individual desires are subject to each individual's own test of the justice of her actions" (p. 169). She goes on to state that Rawls' account therefore creates "a regulatory sense of justice which assesses and controls first-order desires" (p. 169). In both accounts, the capacity to be reasonable is used as a mechanism of control or limitation over individuals' pursuit of their conception of the good. In Rawls, this occurs through the introduction of fair terms reasonableness; it is the fact of individuals as members of a social scheme of social cooperation that demands this type of regulation. In Scanlon, this occurs through his concept of reasonable rejectability. Moore goes on to outline two aspects of Scanlon's formulation which are designed to increase the critical purchase of the concept as follows:

1   Rules are justifiable if they can be agreed under circumstances where no one is deceived or coerced.
2   The criterion of justifiability is based on the reasonableness of individuals rejecting a principle, rather than the reasonableness of individuals accepting it.

Again, this can be seen to add to the capacity for the concept of reasonableness to be used as a critical regulatory tool. Moore states, "Scanlon's formulation, in terms of what can be reasonably rejected, is intended to be a general standard which can be applied to everyone" (p. 173). Again, we can see how the purchase of a regulatory tool based on reasonableness exists because of the nature of individuals in a scheme of cooperation; the standard applies to everyone as all individuals within the scheme are free and equal. Moore emphasises this social aspect as she states, "the motive behind this regulative test is not the desire to do what is right because it is right, but the desire to act in ways that can be *justified* to others who are also reasonable" (p. 169).

So far, this account of reason as regulation has focussed on individual actions. Moore states, "the idea of being reasonable, at least in ordinary discourse, involves the idea of offering reasons for one's action and being prepared to listen to and be persuaded by the reasons of others'" (p. 171). There are two important points to note in this comment. First, as stated, the concept of reasonable we are discussing applies to individuals' actions. Individuals are motivated to action through first-order desires, which are then regulated by the second-order desire of reasonableness. They recognise their first-order desires and then question whether they can justify why these should be pursued to others. Importantly, as highlighted, although they are individual actions, these actions take place within a social scheme of cooperation. It is this scope which places the need for the regulatory test of reasonableness on individuals. Within this scheme, people recognise that they have first-order desires and subsequently recognise that the other individuals within their scheme of cooperation also have similarly motivating desires which might conflict with their own. This necessitates regulation of first-order desires through the framework of reasonableness. The second point from this comment is that Moore, along with Rawls, emphasises the everyday nature of this type of decision-making. Although discussing desires, motivations, and regulatory functions that we as individuals are not necessarily acutely aware of when we are within the process of decision-making, it is this process of decision-making through regulation which enables a just scheme of social cooperation. I will build on this in my subsequent section on Rawls' mechanism of reflective equilibrium.

Moore goes on, however, to critique these constructs of reasonableness at an individual level, asserting that more needs to be done to define the term and to move away from assumptions of moral value.

She questions the accuracy of the description of how first- and second-order desires relate to both each other and other individuals' desires. Moore states:

> Indeed what is 'reasonable' here seems to presuppose a shared understanding of the acceptable line between promoting one's own interests (or not sacrificing them) and considering the interests of others.
>
> (p. 174)

Moore argues that the relationship between first-order and second-order desires within a scheme of social cooperation which Rawls and Scanlon describe is actually a weighing up of the importance of different individual interests. She states, "because only some interests count from the impartial standpoint, the crucial issue is which interests are fundamental (and cannot 'reasonably' be set aside) and which are not" (p. 175). In this case, there is no need to appeal to a social contract so that individuals are in a scheme of cooperation. Instead, there could simply be an outline of what individuals hold as objectively valuable or justifiable interests. There would be no need to rely on a construct of what is reasonable as a regulatory mechanism on desires, as in order to describe what can be justifiable there would simply be a list of acceptable interests available.

Moore argues that the construction of 'reasonableness' found within Rawls and Scanlon's work relies heavily on their specific conception of the person. Because of this, what can be deemed reasonable within these accounts can be seen to include an implicit moral framework and as such "the critical purchase of the 'reasonable rejectability' criterion is achieved by incorporating moral assumptions…into the conception of what is 'reasonable'" (p. 175). Moore argues that due to this inclusion of moral criteria within the concept of what is reasonable, the framework only has critical purchase through "transcendentalising the self" (p. 177). If this concept of justifiable principles or actions is to be reflective of how individuals actually make decisions, then there only needs to be a list of fundamental justifiable interests for individuals in society. This does not need to rely on a social contract construct of individuals in a scheme of cooperation. If Rawls' and Scanlon's conception of reasonableness is to be used, then it does not give a reflection of how individuals actually are and how they make decisions. This framework relies on an account of 'transcendentalised' individuals, with implicit moral values built into the concept of what is reasonable.

I reject this criticism, however. By focussing on Rawls' political account of fair terms reasonableness, I suggest that we can have an account of reasonableness as a regulatory tool whilst avoiding the issue of the 'transcendentalised' self. Rawls' account asks individuals what the limits of reasonable sacrifice are for individuals within scheme of social cooperation operating as political agents. I will go on to show that Rawls' emphasis on constitutional essentials and matters of basic justice can give us a political framework by which to understand where these limits are. This does not entail a focus on moral motivation or decision-making by individuals, but a boundary set upon individual action through the fact of the existence of a social scheme of cooperation. The focus on constitutional essentials and matters of basic justice can be seen to create that framework for a public social world, without reliance on an account of moral values.

A political conception of justice

Within *Political Liberalism* Rawls draws a distinction between comprehensive doctrines and a political conception of society. It is this distinction which enables me to reject Moore's critique of the account of reasonable as regulatory and build my argument for a policy test based on this concept. Rawls outlines that the fundamental difference between a comprehensive doctrine and a political conception is that of scope. A comprehensive doctrine includes "conceptions of what is of value in human life, and ideals of personal character, as well as ideals of friendship and of familial and associational relationships" (1996, p. 13). Rawls describes a comprehensive doctrine (of any kind, religious, philosophical, and moral) as part of what can be described as the 'background culture' of civil society. This focusses on associational relationships such as church groups, clubs and teams, rather than political ones. Rawls states, "the political is distinct from the associational, which is voluntary in ways that the political is not" (1996, p. 137). A political conception therefore, "tries to elaborate a reasonable conception of the basic structure alone and involves, so far as possible, no wider commitment to any other doctrine" (1996, p. 13). This conception does not relate to broader moral values outside the scope of individuals as purely members of a social scheme of cooperation, and the basic structure which supports this. Rawls' account of the basic structure includes society's main political, social, and economic institutions, and how these work together to form a public, social, framework for society. The basic structure on the Rawlsian account is therefore the institutional framework which supports and

enables individuals to live as members of a social scheme of cooperation, with the political obligations that that brings. It is to this that the
regulatory function of reasonableness applies.

It is important to note here how the use of the reasonable as a regulatory mechanism functions within this specific context. I have outlined
that in both Rawls' and Scanlon's accounts, the concept of the reasonable (or the conception of justice) can be seen as having a mitigating
impact on the first-order desires of individuals pursuing their conception of the good. When looking at the scope to which this applies, and
why a political conception of justice is more appropriate for a scheme of
social cooperation than a reasonable comprehensive doctrine, we must
consider the impact of the basic structure on individuals. Rawls states:

> The institutions of the basic structure have deep and long term
> social effects and in fundamental ways shape citizens' character
> and aims, the kinds of persons they are and aspire to be.
>
> (1996, p. 68)

The idea here is that institutions or practices within the basic structure
have such a fundamental impact on individuals' lives that they can affect their agency. It is crucial, then, that decisions taken which relate to
these fundamental aspects of society are properly regulated. The concept of reasonableness can perform this function as it is both one of
two moral powers present in individuals and provides the framework
for the social scheme of cooperation in which individuals live.

Returning to the breadth of impact of the basic structure on individuals, including their agency, Rawls states:

> Publicity ensures, so far as practical measures allow, that citizens
> are in a position to know and to accept the pervasive influences of
> the basic structure that shape their conception of themselves, their
> character, and ends.
>
> (1996, p. 68)

As the basic structure has a fundamental impact on individuals' lives
and is governed by the political conception of justice which is based
on reasonableness, institutions and decisions coming from the basic
structure should also be regulated through the conception of reasonableness. It is this aspect of Rawls' account of a political conception
of justice that I want to emphasise, alongside his account of the liberal
conception of legitimacy.

The liberal principle of legitimacy

Hanberger (2003) argues for the existence of legitimacy capital. He states that democratically elected representatives and bodies make decisions that are legitimate by the very nature of them being democratically elected. On this account, the decisions that are made by elected individuals are automatically legitimate as they have mandate from the electorate to make decisions. I dispute this and argue that decisions made by these individuals and bodies should be subject to scrutiny and not assumed to be legitimate purely because they have been elected via a democratic process. When elected, individuals do have democratic mandate and therefore some form of legitimacy. I would argue that this legitimacy is provisional and still relies on the contents of the actions they are taking or the impact of the decisions they have made. As already highlighted, this is the motivation behind the creation of a test for social policy; that governmental intervention needs scrutiny in terms of legitimacy. Young argues that the initial motivation behind the development of political liberalism was the rejection of the abuse of power and the concept of reasonableness was introduced as a liberal way of providing a moral and legal standard for judging the legitimacy and acceptability of government behaviour. He notes that this standard has been extended over the decades and now applies to the regulation of power "when it is employed to establish and maintain conditions that unreasonably prevent citizens from either pursuing or achieving self-fulfilment" (p. 256). Both Rawls and Scanlon's accounts of reasonableness focus on the recognition of individuals within a social scheme of cooperation whereby all individuals have first order desires to pursue their conception of the good life, and members of the social scheme must recognise this. I suggest that these mechanisms can also be used in the structural context, as described by Young.

We can explore this further through Rawls' discussion of the use of power and the liberal legitimacy principle. In this section, Rawls provides an overview of his argument:

i   Citizens are reasonable and rational
ii   Citizens are free and equal
iii   The diversity of reasonable doctrines is a permanent feature of the public culture
iv   Political power is the power of citizens as a collective body

The question still arises, however, of when that power of citizens as a collective body can be appropriately exercised. He notes:

> This power is regularly imposed on citizens as individuals and members of associations, some of whom may not accept the reasons widely said to justify the general structure of political authority...or...may not regard as justified many of the statutes enacted by the legislature to which they are subject.
>
> (1996, p. 136)

Due to reasonable pluralism – the existence of irreconcilable but reasonable doctrines – being a fact of public culture, issues will still arise regarding the justification and legitimacy of the use of power within the scope of the political society – the basic structure. Citizens can choose not to accept the structure of the political authority that is in power or the specific outputs that the authority has in legislative or policy terms. It is this second aspect that I am particularly focussed on. So far we have seen how individuals have the moral power of the capacity for reasonableness which enables them to have a conception of justice regarding their place as an individual within a scheme of social cooperation. We have seen that this idea of a political conception applies purely to the basic structure of society, and that a particular feature of this political society is that (public) power is coercive. We have arrived at a point where we have stated that due to the coercive nature of this power, there needs to be some standard of reasonableness for the exercise of power to be legitimate. In support of this, Young states, "it is necessary that reasonableness be the 'litmus test' for legitimate public policy/behaviour if the governance framework is to be and remain equally respectful of all citizens and their beliefs" (2008, p. 256).

For Rawls, the 'litmus test' of reasonableness which is applied to the exercise of political power in a scheme of cooperation refers to the constitutional essentials of that society and basic justice within it. When answering the question of when the exercise of power is appropriate in this type of society Rawls states:

> Since political power is the coercive power of free and equal citizens as a corporate body, this power should be exercised, when constitutional essentials and basic questions of justice are at stake, only in ways that all citizens can reasonably be expected to endorse.
>
> (1996, pp. 139–140)

The principle of legitimacy, therefore, asserts that matters of and decisions regarding constitutional essentials and basic justice must be reasonable and can be endorsed as such by citizens. This sets another fairly rigid scope to which the concept of reasonableness applies. I have already outlined the main difference between reasonable comprehensive doctrines and political conceptions as one of scope; a political conception applies only to the basic structure, and not associational relationships as comprehensive doctrines. When looking at the exercise of power within the basic structure then, Rawls asserts that the principle of legitimacy – that structures and decisions can be understood and endorsed as reasonable – purely applies to constitutional essentials and matters of basic justice. I suggest that the difference principle can be used as the 'litmus test' for understanding whether these constitutional essentials and matters of basic justice comply with the principle of legitimacy. In addition to calling on the regulation of government action in terms of legitimacy and acceptability, Young states

> if we are to ensure that all citizens are treated with the respect that they deserve as free and equal beings, then the conditions regulating the use of coercive political power must be acceptable to all those subject to that power.
>
> (p. 260)

I argue, therefore, that the difference principle can act as a suitable mechanism for this. First, it provides a standard by which government intervention (in this case public policy) can be tested against a conception of justice. Second, the principle itself is a product of the original position and therefore has been subject to reasonable decision-making procedures (as will be outlined in Chapter 3). It can also been seen then to be acceptable to individuals subject to government intervention if we are basing the scope of the test on the basic structure. The test is intended to be flexible and responsive to policy decisions, not a single event. In this way public justification for policy at development, implementation, and further iterations and impacts of implementation stages can be subject to public justification. As the test regards reasonableness for individuals in a scheme of cooperation, it relies on practical judgements which are the best available at the time of assessment. The following example can be seen to illustrate this, as well as give a more detailed indication of the difference between reasonableness and rationality.

Applying reasonableness to social policy: the 'Bedroom Tax'

I will provide a case study of a contemporary policy issue here to illustrate the difference between reasonable and rational decision-making, and how policies that relate to matters of basic justice must be subject to the reasonableness criterion due to the nature of their impact on citizens. I will also indicate that my test is a response to a contemporary issue in policy-making; the nature of policy as a con-tested domain. This section will not provide an application of my test but a prima facie illustration of how these concepts might work when applied to particular policy issues. The Spare Room Subsidy or 'Bedroom Tax', as colloquially known, formed part of the Welfare Reform Act 2012. This legislation aimed to reform the benefit system in the UK, which the Conservative Party argued in their 2010 General Election Manifesto had helped create a sense of "helplessness" (2010, p. vii) as "people have too little control over the decisions that affect their daily lives" (p. 63). Instead, following the 2010 general election, the new Conservative-led government wanted to foster active citizenry with a focus on "empowering and enabling citizens to take control of their lives so we create the avenues through which responsibility and opportunity can develop" (Cameron, 2009). The Welfare Reform Act introduced a range of measures aimed at increasing active citizenry and improving incentives to work. The 'Bedroom Tax' in its first iteration removed £12 a week from individuals' benefits if they were living in a house with one 'spare bedroom', and more if there was more than one spare room. Households were encouraged to relocate to more suitable accommodation in order to avoid this loss in benefits. The rationale behind this was to cut the growing Housing Benefit bill and attempt to free up scarce resources by encouraging people to downsize their properties. Individuals were encouraged to move to more suitable ac-commodation in terms of room allowance and were supported in the transition of benefit payment through the use of locally administered Discretionary Housing Payments.

The rational decision-making behind this policy is clear; the new Conservative-led coalition government had inherited a benefits bill that was large and growing, and there was a lack of affordable and so-cial housing to meet people's needs. The 'Bedroom Tax' was created in order to reduce the amount of Housing Benefit being paid out and free up houses that were being occupied by individuals who did not need the additional space. However, there has been a lot of conflict over the introduction of this new measure including a Supreme Court case and an intervention by the UN. I suggest that this measure can be seen as having more than purely a financial impact but also impacting on matters of basic justice. I argue that this policy (as an example of policies that affect basic justice) falls foul of the reasonableness criterion despite being rational. Looking at the introduction of the 'Bedroom Tax' as a matter of basic justice can be seen to show that the measure as introduced fails the criterion of reasonableness and therefore subsequently the principle of political legitimacy.

The UN Special Rapporteur on Disabilities, Rachel Rolnik, visited the UK from August to September 2013 to look at adequate housing as a component of the right to an adequate standard of living and how this fits with non-discrimination. She visited governments, organisations, and groups and received testimonies from individuals on a variety of matters relating to her theme. This included looking at the impact of the 'Bedroom Tax' among other recent changes to the welfare system. Highlighting the historic commitment to equality in access to adequate housing in the UK, she noted "for generations, women and men have progressively given shape to the notion that a dignified life includes access to decent and fair housing regardless of level of income or other status" (pp. 4–5). In the report, however, the Special Rapporteur highlights that the cumulative impact of these welfare changes, and the 'Bedroom Tax' in particular, has led to a retrogressive approach to these rights.

When looking at the 'Bedroom Tax' specifically, Rolnik highlighted that the Impact Assessment provided by the Department of Work and Pensions noted that there was a mismatch between household size and the availability of suitable accommodation for those affected by the 'Tax'. As the properties for individuals to downsize to were largely not available, if individuals chose to remain in their existing homes they were left with fewer benefits than previously, and testimonies reported individuals having to choose between heating their homes or eating adequately with individuals left feeling "tremendous despair" (p. 13). For those who were able to avoid the loss of benefits and move properties, Rolnik stated "many felt targeted and forced to give up their neighbourhoods, their carers, and their safety nets" (p. 12). Rather than the simple pragmatic transaction of moving to a house that is more suitably sized, individuals were having to leave areas where they had family and broader support networks, which in turn impacted on their well-being in a number of ways. We can see what might be portrayed as the rational decision-making that led to the introduction of this measure has had a far bigger impact on individuals in terms of basic justice than recognised by decision-makers. On the one hand, individuals were staying in the house and area that they called home but were having to choose between affording basic essentials such as food and heating, whereas on the other hand they were moving away from support networks, jobs, or carers to be able to afford these basic essentials. Furthermore, in the light of further data on the impact of the measure the savings that had been predicted are likely to be much less than stated as additional support costs had not been considered.

In the conclusion of her study, Rolnik stated:

> Some population groups are particularly affected by the cumulative impact of the various policies and reforms mentioned above. Numerous testimonies corroborated the view that people 'felt squeezed from all sides' in their housing and human rights situation.
>
> (p. 16)

She highlighted a range of groups for whom the cumulative changes to the UK welfare system introduced by the then coalition government were having and would likely to continue to have a high impact. These groups can be seen to be some of the most vulnerable in society and include low-income individuals and households, homeless individuals, and disabled people. The 'Bedroom Tax' affected the first and last of these groups substantially. Research from the National Housing Federation on the impact of the 'Tax' after four weeks of implementation in Merseyside showed that more than 14,000 households fell into arrears with their rent after the introduction of the measure. Of these, it was the first time that 6,000 had ever gone into arrears (p. 16).

Regarding the cumulative welfare changes, the UN report states, "the plight of persons with disabilities deeply touched the Special Rapporteur" (p. 16). Specifically, there were particular issues around the lack of responsiveness of the 'Bedroom Tax' to the needs of disabled people. Many individuals were told that a room where they stored medical equipment or a separate bedroom for a partner or carer was counted as 'spare rooms' and therefore subject to the 'Tax'. This meant that individuals were often being asked to choose between leaving specially adapted homes, or homes where there was a space for a carer to provide overnight care, or being significantly financially worse off. Rolnik stated "at the root of many testimonies lies the threat to a hard-won right to live independently" (p. 16). She noted that these testimonies also often referred to anxiety, stress, and suicidal thoughts as a result of these changes. Rolnik highlighted that previous concerns about the cumulative changes to housing benefit and the impact on disabled people had been raised by the House of Lords and House of Commons Joint Committee on Human Rights. They stated "the range of reforms proposed...risk interacting in a particularly harmful way for disabled people...as a result, there seems to be a significant risk of retrogression of independent living" (p. 17). It is clear, therefore, that the policy had a particular impact on some of the most vulnerable in society due to the very nature of their vulnerability.

The emphasis on retrogression is also important in the context of using the difference principle as a test on social policy. In her recommendations, Rolnik emphasised this issue of retrogression, noting that states are bound to provide an equal or better level of an enjoyment of a right such as adequate housing. She noted some of the policies in the UK that had enabled the enjoyment of adequate housing "are being eroded and the structural shape of the housing sector has changed to the detriment of the most vulnerable" (p. 20). The difference principle states that inequality is acceptable within a scheme of social cooperation if it makes the worst off better off. We can see the two key elements of the principle at play here; the policy impacting on the most vulnerable, and interventions making individuals worse off. As outlined by Rolnik, the 'Bedroom Tax' has a particular impact on some of the most vulnerable, or worst off, groups in society; disabled people and low-income households. The 'Tax' has also been criticised for being retrogressive and withdrawing some of the freedoms individuals have gained around independent living. The difference principle states that the worst off should not be made worst off through inequality. When we are looking at the principle as a test for social policy, according to the liberal principle of legitimacy, we can see that this policy does make the worst off groups worse off. As a recommendation within the report, Rolnik calls for the immediate suspension of the policy and for there to be a full evaluation of its negative impact on the right to adequate housing and the general well-being of vulnerable individuals.

The response from the UK Government to the publication of the report was robust. The Housing Minister at the time, Kris Hopkins (Butler and Gentleman, 2014), called for the report's findings to be rejected stating "this partisan report is completely discredited, and it is disappointing that the United Nations has allowed itself to be associated with a misleading Marxist diatribe". This position was supported by a spokesperson for the Department of Work and Pensions (Butler and Gentleman, 2014), who asserted "this report is based on anecdotal evidence and the conclusion was clearly written before any research was actually completed". We can see here, then, the contested nature of not only policy development but the impact of policy once implemented. Not only is there a lack of clarity between the rational and reasonable elements of the creation of this policy but also the evidence on the impact of the worst off in society because of this policy is also contested.

The example of the 'Bedroom Tax' has outlined the terrain in which my test is to function and has highlighted two key areas of contestation. First, it has shown that there are some instances in which seemingly rational policy decisions actually impact on matters of basic justice. In regard to this policy, disproportionate burdens were placed onto a relatively small group of individuals which impacted on their ability to live independently or pursue their conception of the good. In these instances, I argue that they become subject to the test of public justifiability based on reasonableness. Second, it has shown the contested nature of the impact of the policy on the least advantaged in society. This lack of clarity demonstrates that a policy test that assesses the impact of intervention on the lives of the worst off in terms of basic justice would have some role to play in current debates around policy.

On this account, therefore, there is a continuum of policy where policy that sits in different places on the scale has a different relationship to the concept of basic justice. First, there are policies that have a clear impact on matters of basic justice and constitutional essentials, for example, homelessness policy. There is an obvious interaction here between the policy and the capacity for individuals to be effective agents. Second, there are policies that may or may not have an impact on basic justice. Some other areas of housing policy can be seen to fit into this; standards in the Private Rented Sector or policy relating to the quality of social housing. In these cases, whether the policy relates to basic justice depends on its impact. Finally, other policies might not affect the issue of basic justice at all, such as the protection of historic buildings. It is only the first set of policies that do impact on matters of basic justice that are subject to the test. Therefore, the first two categories outlined on the continuum would be tested; the first because they clearly relate to basic justice and the second so as to understand whether there is any impact on basic justice, and therefore if they are subsequently subject to the test. The third set is not subject to the test as its impact relates to aspects other than effective agency.

In the next chapter, I will further outline my argument for the difference principle to be used as this test. Prior to that, I want to emphasise the scope in which a test should apply. I have argued that the 'Bedroom Tax' policy is actually a matter of basic justice rather than ordinary policy-making. There are two distinct types of policy on this account therefore; those subject to the test of reasonableness and those which are not. According to Rawls' account of political legitimacy, those subject to the test are policies which impact on matters of basic justice or constitutional essentials. Outputs of government which do not focus on these are not subject to the test in the same way. This relates back to Rawls' emphasis on the impact that institutions of the basic structure can have on individuals in terms of agency. Policies created within the basic structure have the potential to support, undermine, or change individuals' life chances. This needs to be recognised through the scrutiny of government according to the liberal principle of legitimacy. We can draw a distinction, therefore, between basic justice policy-making and everyday policy-making. The first type can be seen to encapsulate policies such as the 'Bedroom Tax' as discussed earlier. The second can be seen to be a more banal form of policy-making which does not impact on matters of basic justice. This could include the provision of bike lanes on certain roads, the rate of National Insurance contributions, or some forms of agricultural subsidy. As policies, these have a very different type of impact on individuals' lives than policies such as the one discussed earlier. Rawls' account of the reasonable can be seen to both delineate these two types of policy and outline the argument for the principle of justifiability to apply to basic justice policy-making. In the next chapter, I will outline Rawls' concept of justice as fairness and the difference principle in particular. I will argue that it is this mechanism that should be used as the justifiability test for basic justice policy and will suggest a revision to the mechanism based on an account of agency.

3 A Rawlsian account of justice

This chapter outlines that Rawls' account of justice as fairness, and his tool of the difference principle in particular, is one way of giving an account of social justice in social policy based on the concept of effective agency.

Justice as fairness

In *A Theory of Justice*, Rawls outlines his procedural account of justice for a well-ordered society from within the social contract tradition as a response to the utilitarian account. He describes the traditional aim of the contract theory as (1974, p. 142) "to provide an account of justice that is both superior to Utilitarianism and a more adequate basis for a democratic society".

Rawls attempts to create a procedural account by which representatives within his social contract mechanism can create a substantive theory of justice for their societies. Two key mechanisms of the theory have already been outlined in the discussion on reasonableness; the social scheme of cooperation and the basic structure. Both form key underpinnings of his theory of justice. For Rawls, there is a special relationship between individuals in a scheme of cooperation. These individuals relate to one another as citizens with ties of political obligation based on the moral power of reasonableness, not as individuals within interrelationships. A procedural theory of justice applies just to these ties of political obligation and matters arising from this, not any further interactions between individuals. This, in turn, underpins his account of the basic structure: the arena wherein the theory of justice as fairness can apply. Rawls states (1999, p. 6):

> The primary subject of justice is the basic structure of society, or more exactly, the way in which the major social institutions

distribute fundamental rights and duties and determine the division of advantages from social cooperation.

As outlined in the chapter on reasonableness, Rawls describes the basic structure as the arena in which the principles of justice can be used as a corrective instrument against natural inequalities. This structure includes areas such as the protection of liberty of conscience and competitive markets and comprises therefore all aspects of society which enable basic needs to be met. Rawls asserts (1999, pp. 6–7), "taken together as one scheme, the major institutions define men's rights and duties and influence their life prospects, what they can expect to be and how well they can hope to do".

Building on these two key concepts, there are two preliminary aspects of the construction of this account of justice; a form of social contract (the original position) and intuitive ideas about justice. Together, these form the initial situation by which representatives of the social scheme of cooperation would choose principles of justice to regulate their scheme. Justice as fairness, therefore, is a contractarian approach to justice as it focusses on reasonable agreement of individuals within a hypothetical decision-making procedure. To begin, Rawls outlines an intuitive idea about justice (1999, p. 3): "justice is the first virtue of social institutions, as truth is of systems of thought...Laws and institutions no matter how efficient and well-arranged must be reformed or abolished if they are unjust". On this account, Rawls assumes that all representatives have this initial intuition about justice; that their scheme of cooperation should be underpinned by just institutions.

The hypothetical original position adopts this initial intuition about justice and social cooperation. In this position, representatives are present from the different positions in society. These people are subject to the 'veil of ignorance' where they are unaware of the particularities of their positions such as talents, economic and social position, and how these relate to society. Rawls asserts that this lack of information enables the representatives to make objective decisions about how their society should be ordered as they could be equally the best or worst off in that community. The decisions taken, then, should be free from subjective interests as no one is aware of their standing, wealth, or background. Rawls states (1999, p. 16), "it seems reasonable and generally acceptable that no one should be advantaged or disadvantaged by natural fortune or social circumstances in the choice of principles". If individuals had knowledge about their own particularities, principles could be rationally accepted which reflect their knowledge of circumstances and impact on individuals, but which are irrelevant from the standpoint of justice. Rawls gives the example of arrangements regarding tax in the scheme of cooperation: if individuals knew they were wealthy, they could rationally support measures which would limit the amount of tax paid by wealthy individuals, to the detriment of society receiving services that would be paid for through this tax collection. If the individual knew they had fewer financial resources instead, they could rationally support the opposite measures ensuring that tax collection from wealthy individuals is set at a high level in order to ensure redistribution to those with fewer resources. The difference in decision-making by this individual based on self-interest is that which Rawls wants to avoid in his creation of an objective initial situation for decision-making. In order to ensure that objective decisions are reasonable, based on ideas of justice rather than self-interest, the exclusion of knowledge of individual particularities is crucial to this initial situation.

It is important to recognise therefore that on the Rawlsian account all representatives within the hypothetical structure of the original position effectively have a veto on decisions made within the position. It is this inclusion of a range of views (but no particularities) that leads to the Rawlsian initial situation being one of equality. On this account, considerations are taken of all representative parties in society rather than a single, conflated, representative position, which is the case on other accounts. Rawls states (1999, p. 17):

> It seems reasonable to suppose that the parties in the original position are equal. That is, all have the same rights in the procedure for choosing principles; each can make proposals, submit reasons for their acceptance, and so on.

The original position is the procedure by which a theory of justice can be chosen. On this account, therefore, Rawls is using ideal theory to create a procedure by which a theory of justice can be agreed. This procedure produces two principles of social justice, which act as restrictions to ensure that justice is met by the further arrangements created through the social compact. He asserts that he provides purely the procedure by which justice can be attained so that a range of sets of substantive principles of justice could be agreed upon by different groups of representatives.

As outlined, in order to reach these substantive principles, the procedural principles of social justice must be formulated. These Rawls describes (1999, p. 4) as "a set of principles…for choosing among the various social arrangements which determine this division of advantages and for underwriting an agreement on the proper distributive shares". These principles "define the appropriate distribution of the benefits and burdens of cooperation" (Rawls 1999, p. 4) for a well-ordered society to be created based on a conception of justice. Rawls' theory of justice is therefore a response to the existence of natural inequalities. Rawls states that these are not inherently just or unjust but that how society engages with the fact of these inequalities is subject to principles of justice. Rawls emphasises the importance of equality of opportunity in order for justice to be met and asserts that affirmative action must be taken in order to rectify the natural inequality of opportunity. The principles of justice, therefore, are used to mitigate against the impact of these inequalities as these differences are not based on desert or merit.

Rawls outlines (1999, p. 266) the two principles of social justice as such:

> First principle: Each person is to have an equal right to the most extensive total system of equal basic liberties compatible with a similar system of liberty for all
>
> Second principle: Social and economic inequalities are to be arranged so that they are both:
>
> a   To the greatest benefit of the least advantaged, consistent with the just savings principle
> b   Attached to offices and positions open to all under conditions of fair equality of opportunity

These two principles of justice are considered to be acceptable within the initial situation of the original position and are principles that will enable a conception of justice to be established within a well-ordered society. Subsequently, they address the problem raised in the previous paragraph of the arbitrary nature of natural inequalities. The first principle outlines the liberties that citizens in a well-ordered, just society could expect it to uphold. These include political liberty, freedom of speech, freedom of the person, and right to hold personal property, amongst others. Rawls asserts that the representatives in the original position would agree to this principle as these liberties would be agreed upon from a position of ignorance of social position. These liberties are therefore those which all individuals, regardless of social and economic status, would want to experience within a just society. This first principle is lexically prior to the second as liberties must exist before distribution and equality of opportunity can be addressed. These two principles can then be used to assess the specific sets of substantive principles that arise from the compact between representatives.

Rawls outlines (1999, p. 82) the starting points of the representatives in the original position: "each person holds two relevant positions: that of equal citizenship and that defined by his place in the distribution of income and wealth". The second principle therefore ensures that once certain liberties have been upheld, natural inequalities can be addressed through redistribution, and subsequently equality of opportunity can occur. In the context of the original position, Rawls asserts, individuals would apply the maximin criteria (1974, p. 145): the "natural focal point between strict equality and the principle of average utility". This criterion would ensure that individuals, whatever their standing may be beyond the 'veil of ignorance', will have agreed to maximise the minimum goods possible subject to the second principle. Returning to the example Rawls gave regarding decision-making on tax within the original position, with the veil of ignorance in place representatives are likely to choose the level of tax which provides the most services or resources possible to the worst off in society.

The difference principle

As obvious from the title of this project, this work focusses on the 'difference principle'. This is the first section of the second principle which states that social and economic inequalities are to be arranged so that they are to the greatest benefit of the least advantaged. Following from the primacy of the first principle guaranteeing equal rights and liberties, this part of the second principle aims to justify the existence of inequalities in the context of a theory of justice which responds to the fact of natural inequality. Rawls states (1999, p. 72) that "the difference principle is a very special criterion: it applies primarily to the basic structure of society via representative individuals whose expectations are to be estimated by an index of primary goods". The principle applies, therefore, to institutions within the basic structure and ensures that the distribution within and across these institutions redresses the imbalance caused by natural inequalities. The principle therefore allows for inequalities to exist among individuals but provides a restriction that these inequalities need to be such that the least advantaged are most advantaged because of them.

Rawls uses primary goods as the metric for his account of justice and describes (1999, p. 54) these as "things that every rational man is presumed to want". These are goods which are broadly necessary, whatever the rational life plan of individuals, and Rawls goes on to outline two types of these resources. Social primary goods include rights, liberties, opportunities, income and wealth, and self-respect. Natural primary goods include health and vigour, intelligence, and imagination. He notes the difference in relationship between these sets of goods and the basic structure. The former set of goods is one which the basic structure has a level of control over, whereas the latter is not. Although the structure can be seen to have a level of influence over natural goods, the relationship is causally different than that with social goods. Rawls states (1999, p. 55), "imagine, then, a hypothetical arrangement in which all the social primary goods are equally distributed: everyone has similar rights and duties, and income and wealth are evenly shared". He sets (1999, p. 55) this as the "benchmark" for judging improvements or changes to the social and economic arrangements.

Rawls' account of justice as fairness holds that institutions can be regarded in two ways: as an abstract object or as a "realization in the thought and conduct of certain persons at a certain time and place" (Rawls 1999, p. 48). The difference principle is intended to ensure that each institution in the well-ordered society meets the principles of social justice so that equality of opportunity is available. It is in this way that the principle could be used as a test of contemporary policy and institutions. A particular standard for justice has been set: that any inequality makes the least well off better off, and certain policy formations can be tested against this standard. Rawls states (1999, p. 81), "men share in primary goods on the principle that some can have more if they are acquired in ways which improve the situation of those who have less".

Rawls highlights four procedural aspects linked to the difference principle as a means to give further detail about the concept. First, he likens the principle to the Pareto efficiency principle, which states that a system is efficient if it cannot be changed so that some persons are better off without others being worse off. Although Rawls asserts that justice is prior to efficiency, he states (1999, p. 69), "justice is defined so that it is consistent with efficiency, at least when the two principles are perfectly fulfilled". Second, in defining the least advantaged representative, Rawls outlines three main kinds of contingencies as follows:

a   Family and class origins
b   Natural endowments
c   Fortune and luck in the course of life

He uses these to define the least well off representatives from particular groups. The views of these representatives are then included in decision-making procedures to ensure that despite levels of inequality, their needs are met. Rawls gives the example of the 'unskilled workers' as a group and defines the least well off members of groups as those whose income is less than average of those in the lowest social position. Returning to the example of setting levels of tax contributions, we can see that these individuals would have a specific view to contribute within this decision-making process. This needs to be represented to ensure that decisions made can be accepted as reasonable by those who can be understood as some of the 'worst off' in society.

Third, Rawls explains that the difference principle should raise the expectation of receiving primary goods equally amongst the representatives. This ensures, then, that there is an aspect of reciprocity and mutual benefit from inequality. Rawls states (1999, p. 87):

> The difference principle represents, in effect, an agreement to regard the distribution of natural talents as in some respects a common asset and to share in the greater social and economic benefits made possible by the complementarities of this distribution.

Finally, he outlines that people can increase their wealth and resources through free association as long as the difference principle is met so that a certain standard of equality of opportunity is guaranteed. The principle is therefore based on reciprocity and redress in order to ensure equality of opportunity is achieved. Rawls states (1999, p. 86), "the principle holds that in order to treat all persons equally, to provide genuine equality of opportunity, society must give more attention to those with fewer native assets and to those born into the less favourable social positions". We can see here how the difference principle can be seen as a product of Rawls' focus on the reasonable as one of the two moral powers. Individuals have an obligation to recognise reciprocal relationships between members of the social scheme of cooperation to ensure that the worst off are made better off within conditions of inequality.

Applying the difference principle

A further caveat of the difference principle is that it is to meet the publicity criterion: "citizens generally should be able to understand it and have some confidence that it is realised" (Rawls 1974, p. 144). Rawls' difference principle can be used beyond abstract theory and hypothetical choice scenarios to look at policy in the real world. Within *A Theory of Justice* Rawls discusses this usage within his account of the four-stage sequence of how the theory of justice as fairness is made and subsequently could be used. Rawls states (1999, p. 171) that this sequence "clarifies how the principles for institutions are to be applied" through creating a framework for their application. This stage is based on the framework of the US constitution and forms "an elaboration of the original position" (Rawls 1999, p. 172). Key to this sequence, then, is the role of the veil of ignorance. The first stage of the sequence is the creation of the principles of justice within the original position which has already been outlined. The second stage is the constitutional stage. Here representatives are tasked with designing a system for the constitutional powers of government and the basic rights of citizens. This has to fit within the limits set by the principles of justice as formulated in the original position. In this stage, the veil of ignorance is partially lifted, and individuals have knowledge of the national circumstances of their society, the resources available and economic advancement of society, as well as the political culture.

The next stage is legislative. Here, the justice of laws and policies are to be assessed according to both the limits of the principles of justice and the limits set through the choice of a constitutional framework. Rawls highlights that whether policies and legislation, particularly regarding economic and social issues, are just is often subject to reasonable differences of opinion. Rawls states (1999, p. 174), "often the best that we can say of a law or policy is that it is at least not clearly unjust". Focussing on legislation that relates to social and economic matters, Rawls notes that the particular principle of justice that would relate to this is the difference principle. However, Rawls comments (1999, p. 174), "the application of the difference principle in a precise way normally requires more information than we can expect to have". He notes that the application of the first principle is simpler to understand, as it is clear when there is a breach of equal liberties and rights, and this fits into the second stage regarding the constitution. He says (1999, p. 174) that this clarity is "comparatively rare with social and economic policies regulated by the difference principle". My test, I suggest, enables the application of the content of the difference principle without the reliance on the provision of a large amount of information which Rawls outlines in his construction. It takes the abstract concept contained within the principle and facilitates a way of applying this to tangible policy. The final stage in Rawls' four-part sequence is the application of rules constructed in the previous three stages to particular cases of legislation and policy by judges and administrators. In this stage, all information is available to representatives, as this is required to make appropriate judgements on the justice of particular cases.

Rawls states (1999, p. 176) that this "four-stage sequence is a device for applying the principles of justice" and is also part of the process of justice as fairness. There is already, then, a process by which the ideas and decisions of the original position are to be applied to specific legislation and policy. We can see three different types of judgements at play in this sequence. First, individuals have to judge legislation and social policies. This, as already noted, is done in the context that the citizen "knows that his opinion will not always coincide with those of others, since men's judgements and beliefs are likely to differ especially when their interests are engaged" (Rawls 1999, p. 171). Because of this, individuals have to engage with a further type of judgement: deciding which constitutional arrangements are just in order to reconcile these conflicting opinions about justice. Rawls describes (1999, pp. 171–172) the political process as a machine "which makes social decisions when the views of representatives and their constituents are fed into it". This we can see as part of the democratic process; political representatives feed their views and the views of their constituents into decision-making through the legislative and policy scrutiny processes. Citizens in general can be seen to input their views around constitutional arrangements through taking part in elections. The final, and linked, type of judgement that individuals make regards where the limits of political duty and obligation lie. If the first two kinds of judgements have not resulted in appropriate decision-making based on justice considerations, individuals need to decide whether they are obliged to comply with political rules and obligations.

In light of these three types of judgements, Rawls states (1999, p. 172), "a complete conception of justice is not only able to assess laws and policies but it can also rank procedures for selecting which political opinion is to be enacted into law". However, as already noted in Rawls' comments on the use of the difference principle, the application of the principle (in particular) is often indeterminate. Although this procedure is used to test legislation, with the restrictions of the principles of justice and the decisions made in the constitutional stage, it can still be unclear which economic or social arrangements should be chosen. Rawls states (1999, p. 176):

> Thus on many questions of social and economic policy we must fall back upon a notion of quasi-procedural justice: laws and policies are just provided that they lie within the allowed range and the legislature, in ways authorised by a just constitution, has in fact enacted them.

When we consider the arguments made in Chapter 2 regarding the liberal principle of legitimacy and the rejection of legitimacy capital,

I suggest that this use of the difference principle is not sufficient on its own. I argue that by using the focus on reasonableness from within his later work (*Political Liberalism*), Rawls' difference principle can be used as a tangible way of testing policy in the context of social justice.

Justifying the use of the difference principle

So far, I have outlined two main arguments in my work, the amalgamation of which can be problematic for Rawlsian scholars. This is largely due to these arguments being chosen from different parts of the Rawlsian canon, when Rawls himself had revised his views on his account of justice. The first argument is based within *Political Liberalism* and calls for the use of the concept of reasonableness as a regulatory tool in line with the liberal principle of legitimacy. The second argument is that the difference principle as created and characterised within *A Theory of Justice* should be the mechanism by which this occurs. There can be a problematic relationship between using the concept of reasonableness based in reasonable pluralism and the normative claim that the difference principle is the tool by which social policy should be tested for legitimacy. Rawls' position when developing his concept of reasonableness is that a family of liberal political conceptions of justice could be formulated that would meet his criteria for a just society. Shifting from his account of justice as fairness as the way that justice can be achieved in liberal schemes of social cooperation, Rawls argues on this account that justice as fairness can only be judged to be the best conception due to its attainment of the characteristics of a liberal political conception of justice. In *Political Liberalism*, Rawls is no longer claiming that justice as fairness is the singular way to achieve a just society, but that the model is a 'best fit' for the idea of a liberal political conception of justice and could be superseded by others.

The starting point for my argument is the construct of the original position. As already outlined, this provides an initial situation of equality where individuals are unaware of their economic or social standing within society and must make decisions on justice from this position of ignorance. There are two core aspects of this construct that need to be emphasised for my argument. First, when we think about how this plays out in terms of decision-making, we see that part of the process is for all individuals to consider the impact of the decision they are making on themselves if they were the worst off in society. Although these individuals also need to consider themselves as the most advantaged in society in order to decide based on the maximin criteria, it is this inclusion of the consideration of individuals as the worst off in society which supports my argument for the use of the difference principle. On this account then, the views of individuals who could be the worst off in society effectively have a veto on decisions made within the original position. If individuals within this initial situation feel that the proposal on justice that is being discussed could not be reasonably accepted by the worst off in society, then it can be rejected and an alternative sought. Moreover, according to the difference principle and inclusion of the maximin principle, this should be rejected. When we consider this in the context of the concept of fair terms reasonableness, we can see the argument becomes strengthened.

In both *A Theory of Justice* and *Political Liberalism* Rawls discusses the justification behind individuals in the original position choosing the two principles of justice as formulated. These discussions focus on the understanding of individuals as having rational autonomy and the relationship of this to their fundamental interests. In *Political Liberalism* this is emphasised as part of the discussion of the political conception of the person: individuals are free and equal, with a set of fundamental interests which motivate them. The second point to emphasise regarding the construct of the original position, therefore, is that the principles chosen within the original position are those which "enable the citizens...to become full persons" (Rawls 1996, p. 77) through the pursuit of these three fundamental interests.

The first two fundamental interests relate to the two moral powers, which have already been outlined in Chapter 2. Rawls (1996, p. 74) states, "since citizens are regarded as having the two moral powers, we ascribe to them two corresponding higher-order interests in developing and exercising these powers". The first interest, therefore, relates to the moral power to develop and exercise the capacity for a sense of justice. Individuals have an interest in being able to pursue their conception of what is right within a social scheme of cooperation. The second corresponding interest relates to the moral power of rationality. Individuals have a fundamental interest in developing and exercising their capacity for creating and following a conception of the good. Rawls emphasises that within this capacity is the ability for individuals to revise their conception. Rawls states (1996, p. 30), "given their moral power to form, revise, and rationally pursue a conception of the good, their public identity as free persons is not affected by changes over time in their determinate conception of it". Although the ability to follow a conception of the good life is a fundamental interest for individuals in the original position, Rawls emphasises that this does not constitute the whole of their identity, and therefore identity is not affected when conceptions change. As noted, in *Political*

Liberalism he emphasises this link between identity and conceptions in relation to the individual as political. He asserts that persons have both political and non-political aims and commitments, and these two aspects of moral identity need to be reconciled.

The final fundamental interest is that of the adopting principles within the original position, which enable individuals to pursue a determinate conception of the good. As representative parties, individuals in the original position are not aware of the specifics of the content of their conception of the good, but they have a "third higher-order interest to guide them" (Rawls 1996, p.74). Rawls (1996, p. 77) states:

> The aim of the parties is to agree on principles of justice that enable the citizens they represent to become full persons, that is, adequately to develop and exercise fully their moral powers and to pursue determinate conceptions of the good they come to form.

Although unaware of the particulars of their social positions and the content of their conceptions of the good, parties in the original position are motivated by the three fundamental interests to choose an arrangement of institutions, governed by the two principles of justice, which enable individuals to exercise their two moral powers and pursue a determinate conception of the good life. Rawls (1996, p. 77) states, "the principles of justice must lead to a scheme of basic institutions – a social world – congenial to this end".

Rawls (1996, p. 75) goes on to outline that these fundamental interests are "purely formal" in their structure. In order for parties to make a rational decision on the principles that will enable them to pursue their conception of the good, Rawls introduces the concept of primary goods. He states, "the parties evaluate the available principles by eliminating how well they secure the primary goods essential to realise the higher-order interests of the person for whom each acts as a trustee" (Rawls 1996, p. 75). By looking at the primary goods needed for individuals to be able to exercise their two moral powers, parties can then understand which principles would be most appropriate to enable individuals to be able to do this. Rawls (1996, p. 76) asserts, "at the basis of the parties' reliance on primary goods is their recognition that these goods are essential all-purpose means to realise the higher-order interests connected with citizens' moral powers and their determinate conceptions of the good".

We can see here, then, the link between individuals' ability to exercise their two moral powers as the first two fundamental interests and the subsequent ability to pursue a determinate conception of the good in relation to the "social world" (Rawls 1996, p. 77). The link between primary goods and institutions is emphasised: in order to make a rational decision on how society should be arranged and regulated according to particular principles of justice, parties need to be aware of the level of primary goods needed for individuals to be able to pursue their conception of the good. There is, therefore, a clear link in the outlining of Rawls' account of fundamental interests between the conception, revision, and pursuit of a conception of the good and the impact of basic institutions and primary goods on this. In deciding on principles within the original position; "the parties are trying to guarantee the political and social conditions for citizens to pursue their good and to exercise the moral powers that characterise them as free and equal" (Rawls 1996, p. 77).

Previously, I have argued that policy should be tested in line with the liberal principle of legitimacy when it impacts on issues of basic justice and constitutional essentials. This should be done to ensure that fair terms reasonableness can be achieved; that individuals' decision-making is reasonably accepted by other members of the social scheme of cooperation. To achieve fair terms reasonableness, therefore, there needs to be consideration of the individuals who are likely to be impacted most heavily by these matters of basic justice and constitutional essentials. The group that is likely to be most affected by matters of basic justice is the worst off in society. If we understand basic justice to be matters of fundamental freedoms and ensuring the attainment of all-purpose means, we can see that it is the group of individuals least advantaged within society that are mainly likely to be affected by these issues. Within the argument for looking at fair terms reasonableness as part of the liberal principle of legitimacy, we can see that decisions have to be made that will be reasonably accepted by all reasonable members of the social scheme of cooperation. When we look at the formulation of the difference principle, we can see the clear emphasis on ensuring that the least advantaged receive the most advantage from positions of inequality. According to Rawls' revised approach to justice, we can have a variety of mechanisms which meet the criteria of a political conception of justice. However, ensuring that the worst off become better off because of inequality is not a necessary condition within this approach.

I argue, therefore, that the most reasonable test for fair terms reasonableness as a form of legitimacy comes from the difference principle. This principle effectively gives the worst off in society a veto on decision-making through the original position; if the individuals in this position do not see that the decision can be reasonably accepted by the worst off under fair terms, then it can be rejected. When looking at the legitimacy of decisions made regarding basic justice and constitutional essentials according to fair terms reasonableness, we need to understand the position of the worst off within this decision-making process – the difference principle enables us to do this. Returning to the characteristics of a political conception of justice which Rawls outlines in *Political Liberalism*, the third condition is that measures should be in place to ensure that all citizens, whatever their social position, have all-purpose means. There is no demand within this condition, however, that the specific interests of the worst off in society are taken into account during the decision-making process. I argue, therefore, that if we are looking for a test for fair terms reasonableness as an extension of the liberal principle of legitimacy, the difference principle is the mechanism we should use. The use of this mechanism ensures that any inequality is measured against the interests of the worst off, and individuals in these representative groups will not become worse off through the existence of this inequality. When looking at decision-making procedures, therefore, we can see that this effectively constitutes a veto by the worst off in society on policies that can be implemented within the basic structure.

Furthermore, we can understand the assessment of basic justice to include the capacity for individuals to fulfil their three fundamental interests. I have outlined the relationship between individuals being able to pursue their fundamental interests and the arrangements of the "social world" (Rawls 1996, p. 77). Parties in the original position are motivated to choose principles and subsequent arrangements in the basic structure, which enable them to pursue their interests. If individuals are unable to follow these fundamental interests, they are also unable to exercise their two moral powers of rationality and reasonableness. There are two core aspects of the construction of the original position in terms of decision-making therefore: that those who are the worst off in society have an effective veto on decisions which are made, and that the parties will choose principles which enable them to fulfil their three fundamental interests.

Reflective equilibrium

The concept of reflective equilibrium can be used in this context to understand how the idea of reasonableness in decision-making can be applied to policy in everyday terms. This section will outline how the structure of reflective equilibrium enables the tool of the difference principle to be taken beyond the initial decision-making process of the original position and the conception of justice that follows to a regulatory mechanism that can be used as a means for members of the scheme of social cooperation to scrutinise institutions within the basic structure.

Reflective equilibrium is a means to achieve justification for decisions regarding justice. A central debate within Rawls' approach to a conception of justice is how different values within society can be balanced so that there can be a single accepted set of principles within a social scheme of cooperation. Individuals within this scheme will have personal convictions that differ from others in the scheme, yet in order to secure liberty and equality, a set of arrangements or a political conception for regulating society must be agreed upon. For Rawls, reflective equilibrium is the means to achieve this. Roberts (2007) and Scanlon (2002) both give an account of it being used on an individual level to provide justification for our own personal views, and Ron (2006) expands this to an institutional level where agreement between individuals within a pluralist society regarding their social institutions is reached. Rawls (1999) states that the process of reflective equilibrium involves achieving balance between our considered convictions and basic principles from public culture in order to create a political conception of justice. This process enables a balance and agreement to be reached between individual convictions and shows how these fit in to a wider conception of values as part of the social scheme of cooperation. Reflective equilibrium can be seen therefore as a means by which individuals exercise their moral power of reasonableness and is based on reciprocity within the social scheme of cooperation. Rawls states (1996, p. 385n) at its fullest extent "this equilibrium is fully intersubjective: that is, each citizen has taken into account the reasoning and arguments of every other citizen".

By looking at constructivist accounts of reflective equilibrium, we can see how the mechanism can be further understood in terms of two key characteristics. The first is justification: by looking at different accounts of reflective equilibrium, we can see the force of the concept in terms of providing justification for judgements based on reasonableness – individuals are situating their judgements within the context of the judgements of other members of the social scheme of cooperation. The second is the idea of everyday decision-making. As previously noted in my chapter on the concept of reasonableness as regulatory, a key part of this is the idea of reasonableness as a quotidian part of decision-making. Building on the different points of view as highlighted by Rawls, the constructivist accounts of reflective equilibrium emphasise the everyday nature of this process.

On Scanlon's account, the process of reflective equilibrium is delib-erative and necessary in both making and justifying individual moral decisions. It is not purely a process used to create whole conceptions of justice on an individual level, but reflects, and is part of, every-day moral decision-making. Scanlon states (2002, p. 149), "it seems to me that this method, properly understood, is in fact the best way of making up one's mind about moral matters and about many other subjects". Scanlon also notes that the boundaries for equilibrium pro-vided by the structure of the original position are themselves justified through reflective equilibrium. This, in turn, enables the starting points for all sets of principles to be justified. He states that as well as the justification of shared conceptions of justice being social, the role of the conception is shared. He asserts (2002, p. 154), "the function of the conception of justice is to serve as a publicly shared standard for resolving claims against the basic institutions of a society".

Roberts describes (2007, p. 24) Rawls' account of reflective equi-librium as being a "two-way adjustment process" by which principles and judgements about justice are calibrated by individuals. On this account, both the set of principles and convictions, and the impartial original position which mediates between them, are open for revision. He emphasises the common sense nature of the thinking within both the process and starting point of the original position, making indi-viduals the source of this process. He highlights Rawls' claims about the original position being an expository device, not the sole source of justification, and notes that this mechanism has a "heuristic role" (Roberts 2007, p. 26) in identifying the consequences of our consid-erations of justice. This emphasises the specific role of the original position as previously outlined by Scanlon: it enables proposed prin-ciples of justice to be reached within an initial situation of equality. Roberts emphasises (2007, p. 26) that "the deductive argument from the description of the original position is not itself a primary source of justification" but that the "justificatory weight is taken by the process of reflective equilibrium". Justification is achieved when the proposed principles and considered convictions are in reflective equilibrium.

As highlighted, Roberts claims that reflective equilibrium is an in-tegral part of the conception of justice, which provides both justifica-tion for the principles and an ongoing method for revising or deciding about moral questions. Central to this account is Roberts' statement (2007, p. 21) that "the idea of a search for reflective equilibrium as part of a notion of justification involves modelling what are often very ordinary ways of thinking and reasoning" which, most simply, is "an account of the processes of everyday critical reflection used in moral deliberation and argument". It is this everyday method of decision-making which is found in the process of reflective equilibrium which provides the justification for the construction of a conception of justice, as well as more general moral decision-making. Roberts states (2007, p. 22), "rooted in our convictions about justice, Rawls' starting points are embedded in our everyday methods of thinking rather than based on the identification of metaphysical foundations".

It is these notions of the original position as heuristic and therefore reflective equilibrium as an account of everyday thinking about moral decisions that I argue allows the mechanism to add to the argument of reasonableness as regulatory. The process of reflective equilibrium is one which can be used to critically assess a variety of levels of moral decision-making according to wide or narrow accounts. In the next section I will argue that this can be expanded to critically assess institutions. All considerations, however, concern a political conception of justice and thus the role of individuals within a social scheme of cooperation. Therefore accounts of reasonableness and reciprocity are built into the process of reflective equilibrium.

Extending the concept of reflective equilibrium

As outlined in Chapter 2, Rawls states that reasonableness consists of both assessing people's claims on each other and (importantly) on common practices and institutions. I have used the constructivist approach by Scanlon and Roberts to show that reflective equilibrium enables justification for moral reasoning, which is concrete on an individual level. I now aim to extend this into an institutional account through the work of Ron. This broadened account includes institutional outputs such as policy and legislation, as well as the organisations themselves, and it is this form of output that I focus on in this research. I will continue to argue that reflective equilibrium is the mechanism which can make the regulatory notion of reasonableness and, therefore the liberal principle of legitimacy, have purchase. Through this approach, we can assess whether policies and institutions can be seen to fit fair terms reasonableness.

Ron argues (2006, p. 173) that Rawls' work can be seen as a piece of critical theory in which he pursues a "deliberative turn". He states that in his later work Rawls "situates his theory of justice as an argument made in the context of an ongoing public deliberation and not as the philosopher's grand scheme for reorganising society". This is reflected in this piece of work, wherein I use the account of reasonableness largely from Rawls' later work to make determinate the difference principle, which is predominantly from his earlier work. Ron states (2006, p. 174) that justice as fairness can be seen as deliberative in the following ways:

1 As an argument in an ongoing social discourse and
2 Taking the convictions of the participants in this discourse as the point of the departure for the argument

His account therefore mirrors the constructivist account in that the original position is the point of departure for creating justice as fairness, and this is constructed and justified through reference to the everyday moral reasoning of individuals living within a scheme of co-operation. As Scanlon (2002) values the deliberative nature of reflective equilibrium as a form of individual justification, Ron expands this concept of deliberation to justice as fairness on an external, institutional, level. He highlights that it is the role of individuals' everyday moral reasoning – included in reflective equilibrium – which in turn justifies justice as fairness that enables the theory to have justificatory weight.

When this everyday moral reasoning is expanded from an individual to an institutional level, we can see the purchase that the device of the difference principle might have as a test for social justice in contemporary social policy. Ron asserts that justice as fairness can be used as immanent criticism of societies. This theoretical framework can test institutions and both the values they state they are committed to, and the values they actually deliver on. He asserts (2006, p. 175):

> Justice as fairness can be understood as an immanent criticism aimed at synthesizing the moral values *claimed by* existing social institutions into a coherent model of a well-ordered society in order to demand that these institutions *stand up* to the values that they promise.

The role of reflective equilibrium as immanent criticism on this account therefore is twofold. It can first test whether institutions are delivering on the values of public justification that they claim to be, and second, it can test these institutions against conceptions of justice more broadly. Ron acknowledges that it is the inclusion of individuals' everyday moral reasoning that enables justice as fairness to be justified. He also claims that the process of reflective equilibrium can be used to undertake immanent criticism of institutions through a Rawlsian framework.

Ron, therefore, argues that both the content and the method of justice as fairness can be used to evaluate contemporary social institutions. Rawls' set of principles can be used as a test for these bodies, with reflective equilibrium being used to carry out the assessment. Institutions are evaluated according to our own considered convictions of justice: are these institutions fulfilling the just role we as a society want them to? But also in terms of the moral convictions which they claim to deliver on; are these institutions delivering on the moral terms that they claim to be delivering on? Ron claims (2006, p. 177), "the delineation of the institutional structure of society is part of the process of arriving at reflective equilibrium". On this account, the principles of justice, therefore, implicitly contain a certain ideal of social institutions; it is therefore fair to test them against justice as fairness, as well as the ideals the institutions themselves use as justificatory mechanisms.

In order to undertake this process of immanent criticism, Ron asserts that there are four stages of evaluation at which to look at: current institutions, the values embedded in them, the principles of justice, and the principles embedded in these institutions. This process, therefore, moves away from Rawls' initial practice of ideal theory and addresses the critique of abstract philosophy as being disconnected from reality. Instead, "deliberation is understood as a process in which citizens question the norms and institutions that govern their life" (Ron 2006, p. 181). The process first looks at institutions and the values embedded within them. It develops a theoretical framework based on these principles and proposes an alternative arrangement within the institutions so that these are reflected. Ron asserts (2006, p. 182), "putting this idealized mirror against existing institutions is needed as a first stage in order to identify, study, and transform these power dynamics". Justice as fairness interpreted in this way allows for the starting point of political theory to be the reality of contemporary social situations, understood through a theoretical philosophical framework. We can see here how this account fits into my argument for the involvement of philosophers within the policy process. By applying a model which searches for public justification to a policy, philosophers are able to generate new knowledge or a new understanding about the policy. Evaluating whether values agreed upon by reflective equilibrium are immanent in these institutions can then lead to proposed changes to ensure that these values are reflected. Ron states (2006, p. 185):

> Rawls' theory can be understood as setting a forceful agenda for an immanent criticism of contemporary institutions. Understood

in such a way, 'justice as fairness' provides a set of idealizing 'mirrors' that are needed to view power dynamics in society, not as a model for an ideal society.

Ron's account gives us an indication of how the mechanism of reflective equilibrium can be used to understand justice as fairness as having a regulatory function based on reasonableness and everyday decision-making. We can use reflective equilibrium as immanent criticism to assess institutions both based on the values agreed upon within reflective equilibrium and through the process of reflective equilibrium itself.

By looking at the designations of narrow and wide reflective equilibrium, we can give further clarity to this idea. I argue that the difference principle provides the most reasonable mechanism by which to scrutinise policies related to basic justice, and this is based within the framework of the liberal principle of legitimacy: the nature of the intervention of social policy in individuals' lives requires justification, and this should occur within the context of the concept of reasonableness. Here, we can see the test for social policy has a twofold nature; first, policies could be tested according to the values by which they are justified by the institution itself. Second, the policy can be tested with reference to broader conceptions of justice. This can be seen to mirror the distinction of narrow and wide reflective equilibrium. For the first part of the test we are asking whether this policy relating to basic justice is internally consistent; does it meet the values that institution is using to justify this type of intervention? Here the question is whether the justification that the institution is providing for the policy is matched by the outcome of the policy itself. For example, the justification for the introduction of the 2012 Welfare Reform Act was partly centred around the Conservative-led coalition government's desire to ensure that individuals are autonomous and have control and responsibility for their lives (Cameron, 2012). When looking at the outcome of this project, we can see that many individuals were given less control over their lives following the implementation of this piece of legislation (Power et al., 2014). The justificatory mechanism of arguing that the changes will create autonomy and agency for individuals is therefore undermined by the impact of the policy when implemented. We can see how this reflects the justificatory mechanism of narrow reflective equilibrium which asks whether individuals' considered convictions and the proposed principles of justice are internally consistent.

Returning to the concept of wide reflective equilibrium, this asks whether the individuals' considered convictions and the relationship these have to proposed principles fit within broader considerations of justice. On the second configuration of the test, therefore, we can extend the assessment of the policy to broader conceptions of justice. If the policy matches questions regarding narrow reflective equilibrium and is internally consistent, we can see whether the impact of the policy fits with our wider commitments to values regarding justice. For example, when looking at justifications for policies such as the Right to Buy scheme, which can be seen to immediately lead to greater autonomy and control for individuals who shift from tenants to homeowners, we can look at the relationship between the longer-term impact on social housing of this policy and particular conceptions of justice. This can be seen as an extension of Ron's concept of a using reflective equilibrium to assess institutions. In addition to assessing them for internal equilibrium, as Ron suggests, my test analyses how policy outputs sit within wider discussions of basic justice.

On this extended account, therefore, the actors involved in the process of reaching reflective equilibrium (both narrow and wide) have changed. In the Rawlsian and constructivist accounts, reflective equilibrium is to be achieved either by or between individuals as members of the social scheme of cooperation. In my account, the actors involved are individual or a collective of members of the social scheme of cooperation and the institutions which constitute the basic structure. By using reflective equilibrium in this way, I can show how policies related to matters of basic justice can be scrutinised by citizens within the scheme of social cooperation. There are two ways in which this testing can happen – on a narrow or wide account. Rawls states that the justice of laws and policies should be assessed from the perspective of the agreed upon political conception of justice. By shifting the arena in which the framework of narrow and wide reflective equilibrium applies, we can provide a more tangible account of how this might happen. On my revised account, both the internal justificatory values and how these values relate to the external environment can be assessed.

4 Primary goods
An appropriate metric?

A focus on a metric is important in order to be able to provide inter-personal comparisons based on distribution. When analysing whether a policy meets demands of basic justice, we first need to be able to understand whether the policy is one of basic justice. Second, if it is, we need to understand the impact that this policy will have on individuals. It is crucial, then, that the metric that we use within our assessment of policy is correct. If arguing for the legitimacy of policy based on what it enables the worst off individuals to do and be, we need to be able to measure this. This section will therefore look at accounts which assert that the primary goods metric used by Rawls is not the appropriate measurement of justice. I will assess the alternatives provided, before outlining my own modified metric. Within this theoretical framework I focus on basic justice for the worst off in society; my metric needs to be able to provide an account of this within policy terms.

There is a wealth of engagement with Rawls' concept of primary goods which Daniels (1985) characterises as a discussion of what the target of our egalitarian concerns should be. He outlines that there are three different responses to this question. First, some theorists emphasise the importance of ensuring equality of opportunity for welfare. This can be seen in the work of Arneson (1990) and Cohen (2000). Second, theorists have argued that the important factor to measure is not welfare satisfaction but whether individuals receive the resources they need to pursue their ends. This line of argument is proposed by Dworkin (1981) and Rawls (1999). The final answer focusses on the relationship between individuals and resources in the form of capabilities; what individuals are able to be and do. I argue that Rawls' concept of the primary goods metric does not have to be wholly rejected for my focus on effective agency to work. I will propose, however, that a simplification of primary goods with an emphasis on capabilities is a more appropriate measurement of social justice in social policy.

Criticisms of primary goods

Within *A Theory of Justice* Rawls defines (1999, p. 79) primary goods as "things which it is supposed a rational man wants, whatever else he wants". He states that, regardless of what an individual's rational plans are for life, there are some goods which they can be expected to prefer more of rather than less. He asserts (1999, p. 79), "with more of these goods men can generally be assured of greater success in carrying out their intentions and in advancing their ends, whatever these ends may be". This account is modified slightly in *Political Liberalism* where Rawls gives an account of primary goods as those which democratic (rather than rational) people are expected to want. As we have already seen, these primary goods enable parties in the original position to decide on which principles would best support them in creating a determinate conception of the good. Rawls distinguishes between natural and social primary goods. Both of these categories are those which rational individuals are expected to want, but obligations relating to the provision of these different goods vary. Natural primary goods are those which, although influenced by the basic structure, are not altogether under its control. These include goods such as health and vigour, intelligence, and imagination. Primary social goods are those which the basic structure does have direct control over, and therefore the obligation to measure and deliver these goods falls on this combination of institutions. These include the broad categories of rights, liberties and opportunities, and income and wealth. As his argument develops throughout *A Theory of Justice*, Rawls goes on to include self-respect as a final broad category of social primary goods. He highlights that these categories, clearly connected to the basic structure as rights, liberties, and opportunities, are (1999, p. 79) "defined by the rules of major institutions", and these institutions also regulate the distribution of income and wealth. These social primary goods, then, enable individuals to follow their rational life plan and conception of the good. Rawls states (1999, p. 80), "we are to suppose...that each individual has a rational plan of life drawn up subject to the conditions that confront him". Individuals are happy, then, when they are able to pursue this rational plan and achieve their conception of the good.

The basic structure facilitates the distribution of social primary goods to enable this to happen in line with the two principles of justice. There must be, then, a fair distribution of primary goods between individuals but one that relates to individuals' conception of the good. This distribution occurs within the boundaries of individuals as part of a social scheme of cooperation. Rawls states (1974, p. 553), "there is an understanding among members of a well-ordered society that as citizens they will press claims only for certain kinds of things and in ways allowed for by the principles of justice". He emphasises that the configuration of primary goods is a generalization of the notion of needs, which is distinct from desires and aspirations. This context of a social scheme of cooperation is important here, as conceptions of the good have to be seen to be acceptable under this scheme for there to be a requirement on the basic structure for primary goods to be redistributed. Rawls states (1974, p. 554):

> The institutions and distributions of a well-ordered society set up a just background scheme and a fair principle of contribution for shifting the primary goods of income and wealth so that individuals may form and pursue whatever (admissible) plans they wish in ways that serve their mutual benefit (as measured by primary goods).

There are a number of criticisms of Rawls' account of primary goods, which Daniels (1985) has characterised as a discussion of what the target of egalitarian concerns should be. One focus of these criticisms is the inflexibility of social primary goods to respond to variation between individuals. Variation on this criticism can take two different forms; the first being that individuals are committed to a variety of different rational life plans and conceptions of the good that reflect different value sets. The Rawlsian configuration of social primary goods can be seen as inflexible to this. The second variation is the ability of individuals to convert these sets of social primary goods into the pursuit of their rational life plans or conceptions of the good. The first criticism has been termed the Nagel–Schwartz objection after the initial critical theorists (Arneson, 1990). This outlines that primary goods are differentially useful for the successful pursuit of individuals' life plans. The objection states that the current construction of the set of social primary goods favours those whose rational life plans are individualistic over those whose goals are communal. Arneson writes (1990, p. 441):

> Primary goods, even though necessary to any rational life plan, may nonetheless not enable individuals with idiosyncratic, as opposed to widely shared, expensive rather than cheap, or communal rather than individualistic, personal values to have a reasonable expectation of fulfilling them.

The issue here arises of how individuals are enabled by the redistribution of social primary goods to pursue their rational life plans. Should it be the case that those with expensive preferences get a greater amount of primary goods than those with less expensive preferences? Are individuals able to pursue communal goals rather than ones based on individual liberties or resources? Arneson characterises this conflict in three ways: first, he outlines that some individuals' aims require more goods in order for them to be more satisfied than others. He highlights the difference between an astronomer and a poet in the goods they need to pursue their conceptions of the good; a poet needs just paper and pen, whereas the astronomer needs a range of expensive, technical equipment. If both the poet and the astronomer receive an equal share of primary goods, then they could be unequal in their opportunity for satisfaction. Second, Arneson outlines that more complex coordination is required for some individuals to satisfy their final aims. One individual might want to be left in solitude, whereas another's conception of the good might rest on being part of a successful team. Again, satisfaction of this conception of a good life is based on a different configuration of resources. Finally, Arneson suggests that an individual's conception of the good might be linked to passing on values to different generations. If your final aim is to do all you can to combat the impact of climate change, educating future generations about a particular value set is part of this. Arneson states that this could lead to concerns over fair socialization practices or fair preference formation. It can be argued, therefore, that the Rawlsian account of primary goods favours some conceptions of the good over others.

Outlining Rawls' response to this issue, Arneson notes that Rawls rejects this critique as a valid objection as the basic preference of individuals should not be seen as afflictions that the redistribution of primary goods has to address but as within individuals' voluntary control. Returning to the context of individuals being in relationship with each other as citizens within a scheme of social cooperation, Rawls emphasises the role of responsibility in relation to the creation of a conception of the good. He states (1974, p. 553) that implicit in the conception of primary goods is the position that "since we view persons as capable of mastering and adjusting their wants and desires, they are held responsible for doing so (assuming that the principles of justice are fulfilled.)" Society, in the form of the basic structure, enables and regulates the distribution of certain liberties and opportunities, as well as the provision of primary goods. Individuals who are part of this society then have the responsibility to form and revise their final aims and preferences accordingly. On Rawls' account, then, individuals are able to choose and revise their preferences in keeping with the distribution of primary social goods. Due to this, the issue of the inflexibility of Rawls' account of social primary goods does not arise as if individuals are unable to pursue their conception of the good with the set of primary goods distributed according to the principles of justice, then this conception can be revised.

The second issue of flexibility relates to the ability of individuals to convert the primary social goods they receive into the means by which to pursue their conception of the good. This is the focus of the capabilities theorists' objections. Both Nussbaum (2006) and Sen (1979) criticise Rawls' theory for excluding certain groups within his scope of justice which, they state, undermines his ability to deliver justice on this model. For Sen, this problem is manifested through Rawls' use of primary goods as the metric of justice. Both Rawls and Sen criticise utilitarianism for providing an inadequate theory of justice. Sen states (1979, p. 333) that utilitarianism is a special type of welfarism which "is the view that the goodness of a state of affairs can be judged entirely by the goodness of the utilities in that state" and adds that Rawls' difference principle also fits into this category. Sen therefore rejects Rawls' emphasis on using primary goods as the metric for justice and states (1979, p. 343), "the primary goods approach seems to take little note of the diversity of human beings". On this account, Rawls' approach is inadequate in terms of ensuring that all people's needs are met in a way that delivers justice. Sen comments (1979, pp. 343–344):

> If people were basically very similar, then an index of primary goods might be quite a good way of judging advantage. But, in fact, people seem to have very different needs varying with health, longevity, climatic conditions, work conditions, temperament and even body size.

Sen asserts (1979, p. 344) that these differences cannot be ignored by a theory of justice as it leads to a 'fetishism' of primary goods and a 'partially blind morality'. He links this critique of the metric of justice as fairness to wider debates about formal and substantive justice and states (1979, p. 350), "a theory of justice based on fairness must be deeply and directly concerned with the actual freedoms enjoyed by different persons...to lead different lives that they can have reason to value". Sen asserts that Rawls' theory fails to do this due to its use of a metric of primary goods. On Sen's account by ignoring the differences between people and therefore their varying ability to convert primary goods into actual life chances, Rawls does not provide a theory of justice which delivers substantive freedom.

Alternative metrics

Arneson (1990) argues for a commitment to egalitarianism to result in the equal opportunity for welfare amongst individuals. He states (1990, p. 429), "a principle of distributive justice in a liberal theory ought to use individual opportunities for preference satisfaction rather than primary goods as the basis of interpersonal comparisons". Responding to the criticism that the nature of social primary goods might create a disjuncture between redistribution and individuals actually being able to pursue their rational life plans, he states that there needs to be a firm connection between what is being redistributed and how that affects the individual. On this account, those concerns around individuals with expensive or idiosyncratic tastes would be addressed. Within an equality of opportunity for welfare, Arneson defines welfare purely as preference satisfaction and focusses on the measurement of the opportunities individuals have to achieve this. This type of satisfaction consists of the availability of an "array of options that is equivalent to every other persons' in terms of the prospects for preference satisfaction it offers" (Arneson 1988, p. 87). The key focus in this approach, therefore, is individual choice. Distributive justice is focussed on giving individuals the means by which to satisfy the preferences that they have chosen. Arneson emphasises that a lack of index (such as that provided by primary goods) enables this position to be stronger in terms of responding to variations between individuals' values and rational life plans. The equality of opportunity approach enables a subjectivist standard of distributive justice to be set, which provides a valuation of resources based on an individual's self-evaluation of their preferences. Arneson states that this focus on distributive subjectivism enables his account to respond adequately to issues around the balance of obligations and values between individual and state. He notes that as his approach is based on self-evaluation, there is no one conception of the good which is recognised more highly than others (as can be a criticism of the Rawlsian model). On Arneson's account, therefore, the focus for redistribution is the equal availability to individuals of the opportunity to satisfy their preferences. There is no index of goods which should or could be redistributed in order to enable individuals to pursue their conceptions of the good but a commitment to ensuring that all individuals are equally able to pursue these conceptions. We can categorise this approach as a satisfaction-based approach to distributive justice.

   The second critique around conversion of primary goods into actual opportunities is responded to through the capabilities approach.

This criticism focusses on the relationship between the individual and resources in terms of redistribution and asks what individuals are able to do with the redistribution that has taken place. I have already highlighted a critique from Sen (1979) around primary goods being inadequate to provide an account of this relationship. In outlining a response to this issue from the capabilities approach, I will focus on the work of Martha Nussbaum (2006). Nussbaum provides three main criticisms of Rawls' justice as fairness as a whole. Although only the final critique directly addresses the issue of the metric of primary goods, the other two criticisms contribute to this discussion in regard to the construction of the metric for the principles of justice and the conception of the individuals involved within redistribution. This approach can be categorised as capacity-based distributive justice.

Nussbaum establishes herself as working within a Rawlsian framework and recognises the motivation of a determinate conception of social justice as the aim of both her own and Rawls' theories. She states (2006, p. 177), "the philosophical motivation is profoundly similar, since in both cases the principles are attempts to capture and render politically concrete the idea of a life in accordance with human dignity". However, she distinguishes between the principles of justice as fairness and the initial situation which Rawls begins with, accepting the former and rejecting the latter. Nussbaum therefore accepts the outcomes of justice as fairness but not the procedure by which it is created, and she suggests a revision to the metric to allow Rawls' approach to focus on capabilities. Throughout her work she emphasises that she sees her approach as an extension or complement to Rawls' theory but asserts (2006, p. 70) that the "capability approach provides sounder guidance for law and public policy".

Nussbaum robustly establishes her account as one that is to be determinate and applied to societies. She states (2006, p. 70) her aim as:

> To provide the philosophical underpinning for an account of core human entitlements that should be respected and implemented by the government of all nations, as a bare minimum of what respect for human dignity requires.

There are three areas in which Nussbaum believes Rawls to fail on this regard. His use of social contract theory, his account of individuals as already outlined, and his chosen metric. On this account, this initial situation, or circumstances of justice, undermine Rawls' ability to provide a determinate account of justice as they provide an inadequate account of the world. She outlines four main points in this regard. First, she criticises the primary goods metric, instead asserting a threshold account of capabilities. Second, she rejects the use of the Kantian conception of the person, linking this to the acceptability of primary goods within the theory. Third, she notes that parties in the social contract situation are roughly equal in power and ability, which is unrealistic. Finally, she criticises the emphasis on mutual advantage as a goal pursued through cooperation. None of these aspects of Rawls' theory gives an adequate account of the variety of individuals within society according to Nussbaum. If these are the components of the initial choice situation for Rawls, then the outcome of this decision-making process in Rawls' procedural account will also be unrealistic.

Nussbaum states that those who are not part of the decision-making process do not get their interests represented and therefore the outcomes of the process, the principles of justice in this case, do not cater for their needs. She refers to those who have a disability as individuals who might not be included in the initial situation, and therefore not being part of the decision-making process for the principles of justice. She states (2006, p. 33):

> Issues that seem extremely important for social justice – issues about the allocation of care, the labour involved in caring, and the social costs of promoting the fuller inclusion of disabled citizens – fail to come into focus or are explicitly deferred for later consideration.

Nussbaum contrasts the ability for an able-bodied individual and an individual with a physical disability to be able to use their primary goods resources to highlight this issue. She states that on the justice as fairness account both will be allocated the same resources but that the individual with a disability might not be able to use them how they wish. She notes the importance of accessibility of public space and asserts that even though both individuals receive the same resources on Rawls' account, without a suitable adaptation of public space the individual with the disability still has limited choice in what they can do.

Nussbaum outlines her own conception of the person and societal relations to counteract Rawls' claims and gives four areas where the capability conception differs to Rawls'. First, she states that justice and inclusiveness are ends of intrinsic value from the outset of the theory. This is unlike Rawls' social contract situation where there are high demands on the capacity of individuals. Second, individuals are tied by altruistic ties and mutual advantage. This allows for the recognition of a diverse range of values within societal relations.

Third, a person is a political and social animal who shares many ends with others. Finally, the good of others within the society is part of an individual's own good. Although reciprocity is a key feature of Rawls' theory, Nussbaum clearly emphasises the role of individuals as social, as well as political, animals. She states (2006, p. 158), "living with and toward others, with both benevolence and justice, is part of the shared public conception of the person that all affirm for political purposes". Rawls' initial situation, which assumes individual capacity, undermines his ability to make a robust claim to impact on society, as his procedure excludes groups of individuals and some demands of social justice. We can see how this response to the Rawlsian account of justice fits with other criticisms around the inflexibility of the primary goods metric to respond to individuals' differential values.

Staying with the approach which favours an index-based metric, Nussbaum creates (2006, pp. 76–78) a list of capabilities that must be met to ensure respect for human dignity as follows:

1 Life
2 Bodily health
3 Bodily integrity
4 Senses, imagination, and thought
5 Emotions
6 Practical reason
7 Affiliation
8 Other species
9 Play
10 Control over one's environment

She sees this as a minimum account of social justice and describes (2006, p. 75) the list of capabilities as giving "shape and content to the abstract idea of dignity". However, the list is also described as "minimum core social entitlements" (Nussbaum 2006, p. 75) and not a complete account of social justice as there are inequalities above the threshold. Nussbaum outlines the procedure of her account as starting with outcomes – in this case a life worthy of human dignity – and then seeking political procedures which will achieve this. She states (2006, p. 82), "justice is the outcome, and the procedure is a good one to the extent that it promotes this outcome" In the example of individuals using public space therefore, Nussbaum would measure both individuals' ability to go where they wish with their resources and, unless the public space was adapted so that the individual with a disability could use it, this would not be meeting the minimum social entitlements. On Rawls' account, using resources as the indicator for primary goods, the social justice requirements would have been met.

Nussbaum criticises Sen for calling on the metric of capability to replace primary goods to take account of this asymmetry in use of resources. She asserts that this does not go far enough as a resource-focussed account. Nussbaum rejects measuring justice through any single quantifiable standard and states that her list allows for a broader measurement of capabilities. This, she asserts, would give a full account of capabilities for individuals in society and therefore make social justice manifest. She states (2006, p. 176), "Rawls has simply left out lots of things that are highly pertinent to any real construal of well-being and relative social position, things for which wealth and income are not good proxies". Nussbaum suggests that her account of capabilities through a list of core social entitlements is therefore a more determinate account of social justice. It is based on a realistic understanding of individuals and their relationships in society and allows for an inclusive approach to social justice.

Through these two examples, we can see two ways of focussing on distributive justice; either based on preferences or based on capabilities. Both start from the position that there is not an adequate account of distribution given through Rawls' account of primary goods. Both alternative metrics aim to correct failings of the primary goods account but by focussing on different areas of motivation. Arneson's account attempts to mitigate failures within the primary goods account by shifting the emphasis onto individuals' ability to satisfy their preferences. The capability theorists, on the other hand, focus on what individuals are able to achieve through redistribution focussing on the relationship between goods and capacity to act. I argue that Arneson's shift towards a focus on hard goods and preference satisfaction is misguided and does not adequately address the issues apparent in Rawls' primary goods account. The focus on preference satisfaction does not give an account of functionings and individuals' capacity to act. The capabilities approach provides an account based on capacity; asking what individuals are able to do and be through forms of redistribution. On this framework, justice is measured in terms of capacity, and this is a more appropriate form of understanding a metric for basic justice than Arneson's account of preference satisfaction. I will build on this account of capacity within my revised metric.

Revising primary goods

Daniels (1985) states that there are two simplifying assumptions used by Rawls in his account of primary goods. First, that income and wealth can be used as approximations of the index and second, that the theory is idealised for individuals who are fully functioning. Here he builds on Nussbaum's criticism that Rawls does not account for non-compliant agents. In terms of constructing a just theory of health-care, this is problematic as "in effect, *there is no distributive theory for healthcare because no-one is sick!*" (Daniels 1985, p. 43). However, in rectifying this, and including individuals who are not fully functioning, Daniels asserts that Rawls' scale becomes too truncated. Again build-ing on the capability approach, Daniels states (1985, p. 43), "people with equal indices will not be equally well-off once we allow them to differ in healthcare needs". A crucial issue has arisen therefore in us-ing Rawls' theory to address the issues of healthcare. If the primary goods metric is used as intended, then healthcare is not an issue for the distributive theory, as individuals with disease or disability are not recognised. If the scale is broadened, however, to include individuals with impairments, then the metric used does not guarantee equal out-comes. Daniels also notes that merely adding healthcare to the list of primary goods could also lead to the type of interpersonal compari-sons which Rawls rejected in his critique of utilitarianism.

Daniels makes the claim that healthcare should be understood as a special social good, which should be included within the primary goods metric. He defines the type of healthcare that he is engaging with as at the macro, or social, level, of decision-making. He states (1985, p. 2), "the macro level concerns the scope and design of *basic healthcare institutions*, the central institutions and social practices which form a healthcare system". He notes that this includes support and personal care services and outlines the five types of decisions that might be made on this level. First, questions of what kinds of health-care services will exist within a society can be answered. Second, ques-tions around who will get these services and on what basis. Third, who will deliver them. Fourth, how the burdens of financing these services will be distributed. Finally, how the distribution of power and con-trol of these services will be distributed. Daniels is therefore taking a broad, and structural, approach to healthcare with an emphasis on the institutions (in the broadest sense) involved in delivering these ser-vices. It is this approach which allows him to claim that healthcare can, and should, be subject to a theory of justice. He states (1985, p. 2), "because these macro decisions critically affect the level of distribu-tion of our wellbeing, they involve issues of social justice".

Daniels states that a 'right to healthcare' approach is not an ad-equate starting point for an inquiry into just healthcare, and that it must be situated within a broader, systematic theory of distributive justice. However, for healthcare to be included in this broader theory, the type of social good it is needs to be defined. This, according to Daniels, should include its functions, effects, and why it is different in moral importance to other goods. Daniels asks (1985, p. 11), "is health-care special?" To answer this, he asserts two main purposes of a theory of healthcare needs: that it shows how healthcare is special and that it provides a basis for distinguishing between more and less important types of goods that healthcare provides. He begins therefore at a start-ing point of needs. Daniels notes (1985, p. 19) that "a broad category of health services function to improve quality of life, not to extend or save it". Therefore the range of needs that is met by these services is broad and can include the aim to "restore or compensate for dimin-ished capacities and functions", as well as improving quality of life in other ways (Daniels 1985, p. 19). Here Daniels is beginning his ar-gument for normal species functioning. By emphasising capacity and functioning as key needs, he is moving away from Rawls' concept of primary goods as the metric for justice. So far, Daniels has established healthcare within the Rawlsian institutional framework, defining it as a broad good which should be subject to the principles of justice. In his definition of healthcare needs and categorisation of healthcare as a special social good, Daniels relies on ideas of capabilities to establish the concept of normal species functioning.

In order to create a theory of healthcare needs, two key points need to be addressed: that there is something particularly special about healthcare and that some kinds of healthcare are more im-portant than others. Daniels asserts that this can be done through a categorisation of the relevant needs within the theory. He notes these to be objectively ascribable, in that one need not be aware of their own need, and objectively important, that there is a special weight placed on these needs in a variety of moral contexts. He asserts that these two classifications allow him to use a truncated measure of well-being in terms of preferences. In order to further clarify this, he uses David Braybrooke's (1968) account of 'course of life needs' and 'adventitious needs'. The former is a range of needs which all indi-viduals will experience throughout their life course. The latter gives an account of those needs which are based on individuals' particular or contingent projects. He supports Braybrooke's claims that a de-ficiency in 'course of life needs' "endangers the normal functioning of the subject of need considered as a member of a natural species" (Braybrooke 1968, p. 90). This emphasis on basic needs can also be seen to align with Waldron's theory of homelessness as an issue of social freedom.

In characterising needs in this way, Daniels has met his first aim of a theory of healthcare needs: to show that they are ascribable. In order to show that they are important, he analyses their impact on the equal opportunity of individuals. He states (1985, p. 27), "impairments of normal species functioning reduce the range of opportunity open to the individual in which he may construct his 'plan of life' or 'conception of the good'". Daniels goes on to outline this theoretical position in terms of healthcare. He accepts the biomedical model of health that takes health as the absence of disease and disease as "deviations from the natural functional organisation of a typical member of the species" (1985, p. 31). In including healthcare under the metric of normal species functioning, Daniels is making the concept part of the truncated scale of needs and thus subject to the principles of justice. He states (1985, p. 31), "my intention is to show which principles of justice are relevant to distributing healthcare services where we can take as fixed, primarily by nature, a generally uncontroversial baseline of species-normal functional organisations".

Daniels provides (1985, p. 32) a list of healthcare needs to be met as follows:

1   Adequate nutrition and shelter
2   Sanitary, safe, unpolluted living and working conditions
3   Exercise, rest, and some other features of lifestyle
4   Preventive, curative, and rehabilitative personal medical services
5   Non-medical personal and social support services

He intends this to highlight the functional relationship between varieties of diverse goods in healthcare.

In order to make this account of needs subject to a distributive theory of justice, Daniels now analyses it in relation to opportunity. He states (1985, p. 34) that disease and disability restrict an individual's opportunities "relative to that portion of the normal range his skills and talents would have made available to him were he healthy". Those aspects of disease, therefore, that undermine normal species functioning can be seen to undermine opportunity in terms of pursuing a conception of the good. This can be termed the 'normal opportunity range' for individuals, and disease (mitigated by healthcare services) can be assessed on this scale. He notes two points about this scale in terms of subjectivity: first, that the impact of diseases on opportunities is socially relative and second, that individuals have their effective opportunities limited when a disease impacts on a skill that they regularly used. The impact of disease is, therefore, not objectively valued but valued depending on how it impacts on an individual's normal species functioning. Daniels will now use Rawls' theory of justice to show that this theory of healthcare needs generates obligations in terms of redistribution.

As previously mentioned, Daniels' account aims to include healthcare within Rawls' theory of justice through the principle of equality of opportunity. Daniels has already argued that healthcare services are in place to mitigate disease as it impacts on the normal opportunity range of individuals. Here he takes this further to argue that certain obligations arise from Rawls' principles of justice in regard to healthcare. Daniels notes that both his theory and Rawls' use truncated scales to measure justice. Rawls' takes account of primary social goods, whereas Daniels' regards certain basic needs in the form of normal species functioning. In the theory of just healthcare, Daniels aims to fit the two scales together to place healthcare within the Rawlsian theory.

Daniels uses Kenneth Arrow's (1973) work to show two potential problems which arise from incorporating healthcare into Rawls' metric. First, the difference principle would be so robust as to drain resources from all other public services due to the demand to satisfy those with extreme health needs. Second, it would, result in trade-offs between interpersonal comparisons of utility. Daniels suggests, therefore, that healthcare institutions, defined within his macro account, be included in the basic structure of society. As healthcare needs are vital in achieving equality of opportunity, healthcare services are equally vital in enabling this and are, thus, subject to the principle of equality of opportunity. Daniels sees this as an extension of the scope of Rawls' theory for social justice, based on his principle of equal opportunity. Daniels states (1985, p. 45), "healthcare institutions will help provide the framework of liberties and opportunities within which individuals can use their fair income shares to pursue their own conceptions of the good".

Daniels, therefore, uses his claim that healthcare is a special social good which supports normal species functioning and, subsequently, the normal opportunity range, to argue that it should be included in the basic structure and be subject to the principle of equality of opportunity. He states (Daniels 1985, p. 47):

> Subsuming healthcare institutions under the opportunity principle can be viewed as a way of keeping the system as close as possible to the original idealisation under which Rawls' theory was constructed, namely that we are concerned with normal fully functioning persons with a complete lifespan.

Daniels outlines the four different types of institutions which would be included on this account. First, those that provide preventive measures and minimise the departure from normal species functioning. Second, those that correct departure from this type of functioning by providing medical and rehabilitative services. Third, more extended services which include looking after the chronically ill, disabled, and frail elderly. Finally, services for those who cannot be brought closer to idealisation of normal species functioning. Here, Daniels notes, principles beyond justice such as beneficence are brought into play. He states (1985, p. 48), "each [type of institution] corrects in a particular fashion for a type of departure from the Rawlsian idealisation that all people are functionally normal". For equality of opportunity to exist, all of these types of institutions and services must be available for individuals to access.

Before providing a summary of his theory of just healthcare, Daniels notes limits to his account. He recognises that he does not provide a general theory of justice, and that the account he does provide is conditional on "the justice of the principle of fair equality of opportunity, suitably broadened and given appropriate priority, which I cannot offer" (Daniels 1985, p. 55). He further recognises the emphasis placed on the social obligation to maintain and restore health, with a lack of recognition for the role of individual responsibility in doing so. In concluding, he summarises that his account has broadened Rawls' principle to include normal species functioning and not just access to jobs and careers. He states that his account justifies (1985, p. 57) "the claim that healthcare institutions should have the limited – but important – task of protecting people against a serious impediment to opportunity, their failing to enjoy normal species functioning".

Both Daniels and Nussbaum state that their accounts work within the Rawlsian framework but through expanding or revising his framework of primary goods. Nussbaum criticises assumptions within the construction of justice as fairness around what people are able to be and do. Daniels also builds into his theory the idea of functionings and what basic capacities individuals need to have to be part of a just society. I argue that, when answering Daniels' question of what the target of our egalitarian concern should be, the focus should be on what individuals are able to do and be. This can be constructed in terms of capabilities or functionings, but I argue that there is a requirement for individuals to be able do certain things in order for social justice to exist. I will expand on this in more rigorous detail in Chapter 5, but here it is interesting to briefly relate this to Waldron's concept of homelessness as a social freedom. Waldron's argument also revolves around the idea of functionings, and he measures freedom by the capacity for individuals to meet basic needs. As stated, his argument asserts that as individuals who are homeless do not have access to private space to undertake basic human functionings such as washing, urinating, or sleeping, they are not free. We can see, then, this idea of capability to act or capacity to undertake certain functionings can be used to understand particular policy issues which have an impact on individuals. By applying this theoretical framework we can create a new type of understanding of the problem and therefore potentially new solutions to how it might be addressed.

5 Self-command and basic justice

It is this focus on individuals' capabilities, not preferences, which I want to use within my revised metric of the difference principle. Following on from the exposition of both Nussbaum (2006) and Daniels (1985), I argue that this consideration of the functionings of individuals is important within an account of justice. The criticisms of the primary goods metric for ignoring the relationship between redistribution and what individuals are able to do, I suggest, are sound. There needs to be a focus on individuals' ability to act in order to give a full account of the impact of redistribution within the aim of creating social justice. As Nussbaum (2006) highlights, individuals can be given the same level of goods through a just process of distribution, but what individuals are able to do with these resources is likely to differ. The question of justice here then should be what individuals are able to be and do as a result of this distribution rather than whether the process of equally redistributing a set of goods has been followed. As I have already outlined, Nussbaum considers herself as part of the Rawlsian tradition. Daniels too gives an account of how the focus on functionings or capabilities can fit within a Rawlsian approach to justice. Daniels argues that there should be a recognition of healthcare as a particular type of good which should be included within the primary goods distribution process. I also argue that the focus on what individuals are able to do and be can be incorporated within a Rawlsian framework. I suggest that this can be done through a review of Rawls' comments on self-respect as the most important primary good and the focus on self-command that this brings.

Self-respect as a primary good

Rawls states (1999, p. 386), "perhaps the most important primary good is that of self-respect". For Rawls, this concept of self-respect has two key aspects. First, the concept includes a person's sense of their own value: "his secure conviction that his conception of his good, his plan of life is worth carrying out" (Rawls 1999, p. 386). Individuals must be confident that they as persons, as well as their conception of the good and aims for life, have value. The second aspect is that individuals also have the confidence in their abilities to fulfil their intentions, as far as it is in their power to do so. This, therefore, builds on the first aspect; not only do individuals have to have confidence in themselves and their life plan, but they need to be confident that they will be able to achieve this life plan. If individuals have confidence in these two areas then they have self-respect. Rawls outlines that, without the presence of self-respect, desire and activity will become meaningless, and individuals will fall prey to cynicism and apathy. He states (1999, p. 386), "the parties in the original position would wish to avoid at almost any cost the social conditions that undermine self-respect". We can see here how this account of self-respect builds on individuals' three fundamental interests in pursuing justice, creating a conception of the good, and enabling this conception to be determinate.

In aligning this discussion of self-respect with his idea of a rational conception of the good, a fuller characterisation of the first aspect of self-respect can be provided. Rawls states that there are two circumstances which need to be in place for this confidence in individuals and their conceptions of the good to be created. Initially, individuals need to have a rational plan of life in place; they all need to be able to fulfil the second fundamental interest of having created a conception of the good. In particular, this should be one which satisfies what Rawls calls the Aristotelian principle. This asserts that individuals enjoy the exercise of their capabilities, and that this enjoyment increases as the use of individuals' value capabilities increases. Second, individuals need to have their "person and deeds recognised and confirmed by others who are likewise esteemed and their association enjoyed" (Rawls 1999, p. 387). There is a focus, then, on the associational aspect of self-respect; that the confidence that we have as individuals needs to be matched by confidence or appreciation from others to create individual self-respect. Rawls states (1999, p. 387), "the conditions for persons respecting themselves and one another would seem to require that their common plans be both rational and complementary". In order to have self-respect, then, individuals have to fit together into a scheme of activity within which all are respected, and all associations and activities are enjoyed.

Rawls goes on to talk in greater detail about the nuances of this associational focus of self-respect. He outlines the different types of associations that could be constructed, as well as how the Aristotelian principle and self-respect could function on this account. I argue that it is not the focus on associations, here, that is important, but the aspect of the further characterisation of self-respect, outlining the importance of individuals being able to construct a rational plan of life. Although this appears to be subsumed within his further discussion of self-respect, how this relates to others, and how this supports the Aristotelian principle, I want to use this as the crucial point for my revision of the metric for the difference principle. As already outlined, this research creates an account for how the difference principle could be used as a justificatory test for social justice in social policy. This is couched within the concept of reasonableness and a commitment to the liberal principle of legitimacy. I argue that the difference principle can be applied to policies which regard matters of basic justice to test whether social justice can be delivered through these mechanisms. The metric for this test then needs to be able to give an account of how individuals' lives are impacted by policy interventions that relate to basic justice; whether they are able to fulfil their three fundamental interests.

As the subject of the difference principle test is policy related to matters of basic justice, it is then crucial that some account is given of what individuals are able to do and be in response to this policy intervention. If policy is to be legitimate according to the liberal principle, there needs to be some justification for the level of intervention stemming from the policy. As already argued, there is an explicit link between social policy and social justice; policy should be subject to tests for social justice. By looking at what individuals are able to do and be, we can give a good account of justice. The second step of this position is to look at what this type of focus means in practice. This is where the specific aspect of Rawls' argument on self-respect as a primary good, which I have highlighted, can be used. I argue that the metric for the revised difference principle should be whether individuals have the ability to create and revise a conception of the good. Throughout the previous discussions on metrics and how justice in distribution should be measured, the focus was on preference satisfaction, following a conception of the good life, and having the capabilities to do what you want with goods that have been redistributed. I assert that a fundamental stage of this argument is missing from the general discussion of redistribution. It is important to look at Daniel's characterisation of the argument as to what the fundamental target of our egalitarian concerns should be in terms of preference satisfaction and goods being distributed in order to enable individuals to *achieve* their conception of the good. However, this discussion is based on the assumption that individuals have naturally been able to create a list of preferences or a conception of the good. I argue that in regard to matters of basic justice a key question is not whether individuals are able to satisfy their preferences or fulfil their conception of the good but the prior question of whether individuals are able to construct and control a conception of good in the first place. The test, therefore, asks whether individuals are able to follow their second fundamental interest.

Here, Rawls' discussion of self-respect, and particularly self-command, can be useful. In his engagement with the concept of shame, Rawls outlines self-command as an 'excellence' from which other 'excellences' can flow. These 'excellences' are ways in which virtues can be sought "and their absence may render us liable to shame" (Rawls 1999, p. 391). Self-command, then, is a crucial aspect of individuals' ability to follow their conception of the good life and to achieve a virtuous life. We can link this to his emphasis on the importance of having a rational plan of life in order to foster self-respect. Both having the ability to have control over your life (self-command) and to use this to create aspirations and motivations (a rational plan of life or conception of the good) are crucial to Rawls' account of primary goods. There needs to be a primary step, therefore, in our discussion of how metrics around justice and distribution should function. Instead of questioning whether there is a triangulation of individuals' preferences or conceptions of the good, distributed goods, and abilities of individuals to link these two aspects, there first needs to be a discussion of whether individuals have had the opportunity to create a preference list or conception of the good. The question, then, does not focus on whether individuals are able to satisfy their choices because of redistribution, but whether they are in a position to have choices around preferences and aspirations in the first place.

This shift can be taken whilst working within the Rawlsian framework. Built into my position is a focus on individuals' capabilities, which has come from the work of Nussbaum, but we have also seen with Daniels' discussion of Braybrooke's (1968) framework of functionings and course of life needs that this focus can be incorporated within a Rawlsian framework. Unlike Daniels, however, I am not adding extra types of goods to the list of primary goods. Instead, I am arguing that an initial paring back of primary goods is done to address the primary question of whether individuals have, or have had, the opportunity to create a set of aspirations or preferences. This is based on Rawls' discussion of self-respect as the most important primary good and the small mechanism within this discussion where he states that individuals must first have a rational life plan to attain self-respect. By looking at this in the context of self-command, we can argue that there needs to be a primary review of whether individuals have the capability of self-command before discussions around the re-lationship between distribution of goods and enabling conceptions of the good occur.

Self-command and social freedom

To further understand my argument that an additional initial stage needs to be looked at as a metric, we can return to Waldron's (1991) theory of homelessness as social freedom. In his article, Waldron states (1991, p. 306) that "homelessness consists in unfreedom". He reaches this conclusion by looking at the things that individuals can do, dependent on the space that they are able to access. He argues that activities are categorised by the spaces in which individuals are able to perform these, outlining a range of activities which are not allowed to be undertaken in public spaces – only private spaces. These include fundamental human activities such as washing, urinating, and sleeping.

We can consider this analysis in the context of Rawls' discussion of self-command related to self-respect as a primary good. The test here is not whether individuals are free, but whether they are able to achieve self-command and subsequently create a conception of the good, or set of preferences and aspirations which constitute a rational life plan. Waldron has discussed that individuals who are homeless have no access to private space. The only space which they are generally freely able to access is public space; however, there are limitations on the activities which can take place in these spaces. When we think about the impact of this access to space on the ability to create a rational life plan, I suggest that this lack of space for meeting basic human func-tionings undermines the ability to create a conception of the good. I argue that if individuals' situations are such that they are not free to undertake fundamental human functionings, then they are also not free or able to create a rational life plan.

There are two aspects to this argument linked to Rawls' account of self-respect as a primary good. First, if individuals are struggling to meet basic human needs in terms of shelter, warmth, and security, they do not have the luxury of reflection on aspirations. Returning to Braybrooke's (1968) account of course of life needs, it could be argued that individuals who are unable to meet these needs are unable to develop adventitious needs based on chosen projects. I assert that when individuals are using their energy to try and meet fundamental needs, then they are unable to reflect on their aspirations and preferences and create a rational plan for life. Second, even if the first aspect is not true and individuals are able to create a rational life plan, Rawls calls for this to be a realistic plan that individuals can be confident in achieving. Again, the state of homelessness is often a struggle for survival – individuals are working towards meeting basic human needs, not necessarily working to achieve a broader aspirational life plan.

This critique of homelessness and self-command is not intended as a moral judgement or criticism of individuals who find themselves homeless. Instead, it is meant to aid understanding about the relationship between self-command and basic justice. I would argue (and do argue later on in this text) that homelessness is a matter of basic justice, and that the state of homelessness undermines individuals' ability to have control over what they can be and do. I assert that being homeless often undermines self-command, and it this type of matter of basic justice that needs to be analysed. This is also not to say that all individuals who are homeless are not able to achieve self-command. Some individuals may choose to be homeless as part of their rational life plan. For these individuals, their ability to achieve self-command is not undermined by being homeless but is a result of it.

A further way of understanding this position is through a consideration of Maslow's (1943) hierarchy of needs. Maslow outlines a theory of human motivation where a series of needs take a hierarchical form, with each set of needs being largely dependent on the satisfaction of others. He states (1943, p. 370), "human needs arrange themselves in hierarchies of prepotency". This condition means not only does the satisfaction of a set of needs depend on the satisfaction of 'lower' needs, but that the appearance of needs relies on the prior satisfaction of others. Maslow does not intend this to be a rigid definition of needs, but a suggested framework for future research on how human motivation can be understood.

The first set of needs in Maslow's hierarchy is that of physiological needs. He does not present a list of fundamental needs of this kind, but notes that the needs arise as a response to a lack of a physical element of some kind, such as food or warmth. These types of needs would be the most urgent for individuals to meet if they were lacking a number of different needs. Maslow states (1943, p. 373), "a person who is lacking food, safety, love, and esteem, would probably hunger for food more strongly than for anything else". The first point from Maslow, here, is that if there are physiological needs that have not been met for an individual, then it is these that the individual will be most motivated to meet. As previously noted, however, Maslow's analysis also states that within the hierarchy the existences of some needs are reliant on the satisfaction of prior, more fundamental, needs. In the above example, not only would hunger be the most urgent need to meet, but it is likely to impede the development of subsequent 'higher order' needs. Maslow asserts (1943, p. 373), "if all the needs are unsatisfied, and the organism is then dominated by the physiological needs, all other needs may become simply non-existent or be pushed into the background". Again, he returns to the example of hunger. He describes the individual who is hungry as having a consciousness that is pre-empted by hunger. For this individual, the organisation of all capacities is determined by the purpose of satisfying hunger, and all capacities are being used to satisfy this one aim: "the receptors and effectors, the intelligence, memory, habits, all may now be defined simply as hunger-gratifying tools" (1943, p. 373). In the presence of a physiological need, therefore, capacities have been transformed into tools with the one function of meeting that fundamental need.

Maslow also states that the way that the individual engages with the future is also fundamentally changed if there is a physiological need that is not met. He comments (1943, p. 374) that the result of the need not being met is that "the whole philosophy of the future tends also to change". There are therefore two ways in which individuals' capacities have changed. First, when physiological needs are not met, capacities become simple tools with which to meet that need. Second, simple capacities are no longer used in order to consider or plan the future, leading to the development of other capacities within the hierarchy. Maslow asserts (1943, p. 374), "freedom, love, community feeling, respect, philosophy, may all be waved aside as fripperies which are useless since they fail to fill the stomach". We can see, then, how this fits with Waldron's (1991) theory of homelessness as an issue of social freedom. Waldron argues that the lack of space within which basic human functions can be undertaken undermines an individual's freedom. Maslow's hierarchy also outlines the urgency of fundamental human functionings or physiological needs being met. Without these being met, individuals are unable to achieve higher levels of functioning such as engaging with freedom, community, and love. They are also unable to adequately plan for the future.

In the final aspect of Maslow's theory which I want to draw upon, we can see how the Rawlsian account of self-command can fit into the analysis. As with Rawls, Maslow highlights the importance of individuals being able to pursue their conception of the good. Maslow emphasises the role that gratification plays as a motivator in human behaviour. This can be seen to fit with Rawls' discussion of the Aristotelian principle. On both accounts, it is important for individuals to have their needs satisfied in order to develop the engagement with further, more meaningful needs. He states (1943, p. 375) that gratification "releases the organism from the domination of a relatively more physiological need, permitting thereby the emergence of other more social goods". This focus on gratification leads Maslow to develop an argument around self-esteem and self-actualization, which I argue can be seen to fit into the Rawlsian account of self-command. Maslow says (1943, p. 382), "what a man *can* be, he *must* be" and emphasises the role of fulfilment of needs within an account of self-actualization. On this account, individuals must have the freedom to actualize the person that they have the capacity to be and "to become everything that one is capable of becoming" (Maslow 1943, p. 382). The emergence of these needs of fulfilment and actualization, however, are reliant on the prior satisfaction of more fundamental needs such as the category of physiological needs. We can relate this discussion of self-actualization to the idea of the creation of a conception of a good life within Rawlsian theory and the pursuit of fundamental interests. For Rawls, individuals should be able to be in a position to create a conception of a good life, which it is important for them to work towards and fulfil. For Maslow, this is discussed in terms of capacities and self-actualization for potential within individuals.

This discussion of self-actualization and a hierarchy of needs fits into my critique of the primary goods metric. Within Maslow's hierarchy, fundamental needs must be met for individuals to be able to develop needs around more 'higher order' capacities and to be able to engage with the idea of future needs or capacities. This can be reflected in my discussion around the creation of a conception of the good. I argue that there are instances when individuals have such needs that they are unable to create a conception of the good. It is this metric that I argue for in the context of a test for basic social justice. Maslow argues that if individuals have physiological needs that are unmet, then the rest of the individuals' capacities will be focussed on meeting this need – not creating a philosophy or vision of the future. I suggest that the difference principle can be used to test issues of basic justice in terms of policy through giving an account of whether individuals are able to satisfy their fundamental interests and follow a conception of the good life.

The revised metric

My revised metric for use alongside my configuration of the difference principle is thus: the test of social justice in social policy should measure whether the worst off in society are able to create, amend, and follow a rational life plan. This step is to be inserted before discussions on the redistribution of primary goods and is to fit into a Rawlsian framework. I argue that in order for social justice to be achieved, individuals need to be able to have self-command and the ability to create a conception of the good – they need to be able to pursue their three fundamental interests. For ease of reference, I will refer to this as individuals having effective agency. The critique of homelessness allows us to take the first step towards understanding how this might work in policy terms. If my revised difference principle was being used as a test on the issue of homelessness, we could say that a policy which results in individuals being homeless failed to meet standards of basic justice as some individuals were unable to achieve self-command. Remember, it is not that there is an absolutely necessary connection between lack of control and homelessness – some individuals may have included this as part of their rational life plan. However, we can argue that if there are individuals who are homeless who do not want to be homeless, then their ability to choose what they want to be and do is undermined through their state of homelessness.

My argument around this revised metric does not suggest that the primary goods account should be rejected, or that the capabilities approach or any other alternative metric be adopted. What it states is that for my version of the difference principle to be a test for social justice in social policy, a different approach should be taken. It also does not state that the primary goods metric cannot function on my account of the difference principle. The range of primary goods can be looked at from the position of social justice in the context of the liberal principle of legitimacy. However, what is fundamental to the use of the test is that the first metric used is whether worst off individuals are able to create, revise, and follow a conception of the good or rational life plan; whether these individuals are able to be effective agents. When we are discussing whether individuals are able to do what they want to do, it is important to distinguish between those who are lacking satisfaction in the actions they are able to take and those who lack the capacity to act. This can be highlighted through the consideration of the difference between those who are busy and those who are struggling. Both groups can be seen to be experiencing the same problem – lack of time due to having too much to do. However, there is a fundamental difference in terms of self-command. Individuals who are busy have created a conception of the good life for themselves and are pursuing it to some extent, they are able to revise their conception or approach to their conception to better satisfy their choices, if they wish. Individuals who are struggling are not able to revise their use of time and resources. For example, they could only be able to get a zero hours contract and have to work all the hours offered to them at a certain time because they are unsure whether the hours will be available the following week and have rent to pay. The difference here lies within the individuals' ability to achieve self-command.

We have seen how this addition can be justified through the Rawlsian emphasis on self-respect as a primary good, and we have seen how this revised metric can give insight into an issue of basic justice such as homelessness. The next stage of the argument then is to outline how this will work in the context of my test. The following chapter will consolidate my theoretical arguments throughout the initial framework and will outline, in greater detail, how the test will work holistically. Here, I will just give some indication of how the revised metric might work in practice. When looking at a piece of legislation or policy, then, the question will be whether that intervention makes individuals who are the worst off in society more or less able to achieve self-command: to have control over what they want to do or be. The aim of the test is to find out whether a policy intervention that relates to basic justice can be justified according to the liberal principle of legitimacy. It questions whether the policy intervention can be accepted as reasonable by individuals who are affected by this intervention. I argue then, that the metric itself can be seen as subject to the regulatory test of reasonableness. It would be unreasonable to argue that individuals who are members of a social scheme of cooperation should be expected to live without control over what they want to be and do. I assert that it is reasonable to require all members of this scheme to be able to construct, revise, and follow a conception of the good.

Returning to my analysis of the 'Bedroom Tax', I first argued that this could be seen as a matter of basic justice. I then outlined how the policy intervention could be seen to fail the reasonableness criterion as individuals who could be understood as some of the worst off in society were seen to be worse off in a variety of ways due to this intervention. The review of the policy by the UN (Rolnik 2013) showed that some particular groups were likely to be more impacted by the 'Tax' than others, and that individuals' ability to live independently was being undermined. When looking at this in the context of my revised metric, we can understand the policy to be undermining individuals' ability to construct and follow a conception of the good life and to define what they want to be and do. The impact of the 'Tax' included individuals having to move away from family and communities where they had established a conception of the good for themselves and were pursuing a rational life plan. In some cases also, individuals were having to move away from specially adapted houses which had been designed to directly enable individuals to decide on and pursue aspirations and preferences.

We can see, then, how this revised metric fits into the focus on reasonableness as regulatory within the revision of the use of the difference principle. The metric itself can be understood to be subject to the test for reasonableness; it would be unreasonable for individuals to be expected to lack self-command as members of a social scheme of cooperation. We can then use this metric to further understand the impact of particular policy interventions which impact on matters of basic justice. The test would ask whether the intervention enabled or undermined worst off individuals' ability to achieve self-command and decide for themselves what they want to do and be. I have argued that it is unreasonable to expect individuals to lack self-command. It would also be unreasonable for individuals to experience less self-command as a result of a policy intervention. Therefore, if the test finds that individuals who are the worst off in society are less able to make choices around conceptions of a good life or preferences due to a policy intervention, then that intervention has failed the test and is unreasonable.

Crucial to this account is the link between my revised metric, fundamental interests, and the two moral powers. I have outlined that self-respect as a primary good and the related concept of self-command can be understood to be linked to Rawls' accounts of individuals as having three fundamental interests. Interests two and three in this account relate to the creation of and making determinate a conception of the good. The idea of self-command then can be seen to encapsulate these two fundamental interests. When looking at the source of these interests, the second fundamental interest regarding the creation of a conception of the good stems from the second moral power of individuals: rationality. By following a metric which assesses whether individuals have self-command and are able to follow two of their three fundamental interests, we are also assessing the capacity of individuals to exercise their moral powers. If individuals do not have self-command and are unable to create and pursue a conception of the good, then they are unable to exercise their moral power of rationality. The test as created, then, assesses whether individuals have the capacity to exercise rationality or not due to the impact of policy. If a policy either does not enable, or undermines, the worst offs' ability to create a conception of the good, then it is not allowing them to exercise their second moral power and fails the standard of basic justice.

It is important to remember that this test applies to policy which addresses matters of basic justice within the policy continuum. Due to the structure of the difference principle, the focus is on the worst off individuals within society. It is also important to remember that the test does not ask whether individuals have or can satisfy their preferences but is based on capacity; whether they are able to construct a conception of the good for themselves. It does not ask what individuals are able to do with the goods that are redistributed to them or whether there is sufficient redistribution based on preferences but whether these individuals have the ability and opportunity to create a picture of aspirations, preferences, or the good life. It also asks whether this ability has been diminished through a particular policy intervention. As stated, if individuals who are the worst off in society are less able to create a conception of the good or rational life plan due to a policy intervention, then the intervention has failed the test for basic justice.

6   Applying philosophy to housing

This final chapter will outline the final formulation of the test and apply it to a number of policy areas to see whether it has critical purchase. As previously outlined, I have modified the metric of basic justice from primary goods to a focus on the ability of individuals to be effective agents. This can be justified through Rawls' commitment to self-command as a primary good and does not undermine the primary goods metric but pares it back. The focus in my revised metric is therefore whether individuals are able to formulate and follow a conception of the good.

The difference principle states that social and economic inequalities are to be arranged so that they are to the greatest benefit of the least advantaged. I have argued that the existence of social policy responds to both social and economic inequalities as a form of mitigation. I have also outlined that when discussing the 'greatest benefit' within the context of the difference principle, it is preferable to revise the metric to one of effective agency rather than primary goods. What we are testing on my modified account, therefore, is policy (as a response to natural inequalities) and how this interacts with effective agency for individuals who are the least advantaged. This critical approach is based on the framework of the liberal principle of legitimacy relating to matters of basic justice and constitutional essentials. This revision leads us to reformulate the difference principle as:

> Does this policy make the worst off better off in terms of effective agency?

I have argued that the role of social policy, in mitigating natural inequalities, provides a site of social justice and policy which can relate to basic justice and can, therefore, be seen to be subject to this principle. This principle can therefore be used to test social policy which addresses basic justice and/or constitutional essentials to see whether it does fulfil its aim of social justice through improving the effective agency of the worst off.

Within the theoretical framework as stands, we have the following five core elements to inform the test:

a   The scope of the test – policy that impacts on issues of basic justice and constitutional essentials.
b   The negative test formation based on Scanlon's concept of 'reasonable rejectability'.
c   The element of retrogression included within the difference principle.
d   The concept of reflective equilibrium as an example of everyday regulatory decision-making.
e   A revised metric for basic justice – effective agency for the least advantaged.

These aspects have been discussed and highlighted throughout the exposition of my theoretical framework for my test. Although these are not all the elements of the framework, they are the core concepts for my modification of the difference principle as a means to apply the liberal principle of legitimacy within the context of reasonableness.

The modified test

The core assumption underpinning my test, as previously highlighted, is that it is unreasonable for individuals within a social scheme of cooperation to not be effective agents. The test is based on this premise then: that it is reasonable for individuals living in a social scheme of cooperation to be effective agents, and any proposal which would cause individuals not to live as effective agents could be reasonably rejected. The first element of the test is therefore:

1   Does this policy enable the least advantaged individuals to be effective agents?

This first question tests whether the liberal principle of legitimacy can be met; that the interventionist nature of policy can be justified through the positive (or lack of negative) impact that it has on the lives of those who could be considered the worst off in society. Focussing on the negative test format as included from Scanlon's work, if a policy fails the first question, the test does not outline what needs to be done in order to make the policy better. The question purely asks whether the policy delivers or enables the simple standard of basic justice – effective agency.

The second question within the test relates to the formulation of the difference principle and its focus on retrogression. It asks:

2 Does the policy make the least advantaged individuals in society worse off in terms of effective agency?

This emulates the focus in the difference principle on the worst off being made better off despite the existence of inequalities in primary goods. There are therefore two standards that my test engages in; first, whether effective agency is at all enabled by the policy. Second, whether the policy has any retrogressive impact where individuals are made worse off in terms of effective agency because of this intervention.

This test can, then, provide a series of analyses of the impact of a particular policy. First, we can use it to understand whether the policy affects matters of basic justice. As already mentioned, there will be some policies where it is clear whether the policy is one of basic justice, but with others it will not be clear. Applying the test, and seeing what the relationship between the policy and effective agency is, will provide this information before the test can be properly applied. Second, if a policy is understood to relate to matters of basic justice, the test can provide an account of how the policy and effective agency fit together. It asks whether the policy enables effective agency, based on the assumption that it would be unreasonable for individuals within a scheme of social cooperation to not be able to exercise self-command. Finally, the test questions whether there are retrogressive elements to the impact of the policy on effective agency. If the policy does enable effective agency, the test assesses whether individuals are able to decide and act on what they want to do and be as they were before.

Application to policy

The final section of this book aims to demonstrate how the theoretical framework constructed can be used to analyse policy. In it, I will revisit two policy examples already discussed and add a third example to show that my modified test can be used to deepen our understanding of policy in social justice terms. The policy examples provided clearly fit into the basic justice area of the policy continuum that I outlined. All relate to individuals who could be considered vulnerable and also regard housing policy related to independent living, both of which fall under the umbrella of basic justice. Across these examples we will see how the test can indicate whether a policy does or does not enable individuals to be effective agents, as well as seeing whether individuals are made worse off in terms of effective agency through this new intervention.

We can first return to the case of the 'Bedroom Tax' to see how the two parts of this test can function. When applying the first question of the test, we can see that according to Rolnik's (2013) analysis the 'Tax' does not enable individuals to have effective agency. There is no positive measure around ensuring that individuals are able to consider and act on what they want to do and be in the form of a conception of a good life. The testimonials shared with Rolnik outlined how individuals were experiencing a variety of negative impacts from the change. These included physical (or physiological) impacts, such as having to choose whether to have adequate heating or eat adequately if they were being taxed for the extra room(s). Social impacts included moving away from family and support networks if individuals did downsize to avoid the cut in benefit. There were also psychological impacts such as suffering from anxiety and depression related to these physical and social impacts (2013). If we consider these in the context of Maslow's (1943) hierarchy, we can see that individuals were not able to meet fundamental sets of needs, which according to Maslow impacts on their ability to engage with and plan for the future. We can therefore see that the impact of this benefit change did not increase individuals' capacity for effective agency.

Another core feature of Rolnik's (2013) analysis was the retrogressive impact of the 'Tax'. This fits into the second question within the test. Rolnik highlighted that as well as the impact outlined already, individuals were also having their ability to live independently negatively affected by the benefit change. As a result of the changes, some individuals were having to leave specially adapted accommodation to move to unadapted accommodation or rooms were being classified as 'spare' when they were used to store medical equipment or provide accommodation for carers. The impact of this was to remove some elements of independent living for individuals. In this instance then, individuals were not better off in terms of effective agency because of the intervention of the policy, but worse off. The 'Bedroom Tax' therefore can be seen to fail both sections of the test; it does not enable effective agency, and it has a retrogressive impact on individuals.

The second policy area to return to is Housing First. As outlined in Chapter 1, this is a form of service provision which focusses on a person-centred approach to support with individuals being provided permanent accommodation without condition. Individuals are then able to tailor the support that they access to enable them to sustain their tenancy. Bretherton and Pleace (2015) undertook an evaluation of nine Housing First services in England. All of these services delivered open-ended support with client loads of five to ten per Housing First worker. Eight of these services delivered accommodation through a combination of privately and socially rented housing, and all accepted individuals who had experiences issues related to anti-social behaviour, substance misuse, mental health problems, and/or rent arrears. Twenty-seven% of the service users were women, and the service users had been homeless for an average of 14 years. Although experiences of Housing First provision were not universally positive, and Bretherton and Pleace (2015) recognise that they were unable to engage with individuals who had left the services, there were a number of outcomes of interest that were common across the services. A total of 62% of respondents stated that they were very satisfied with their housing, and 26% stated they were fairly satisfied. A total of 80% stated that they felt safe all or most of the time, and 89% said that the service enabled them to do what they want, when they want. In terms of impacting on other areas of their lives, 63% of respondents stated that their health had improved since being involved in Housing First, and 66% reported better mental health. Both individuals' sense of belonging and contact with family had also improved since being housed through a Housing First service. Bretherton and Pleace state (2015, p. 5), "service users saw the freedom, choice, and sense of security from having their own home as the key strengths of Housing First". We can see here clear links to the metric of effective agency; this is a form of service provision which focusses on enabling individuals to take control of their lives, and this is recognised as a measure of success by service users within evaluations.

Although currently still an approach being delivered by different non-statutory organisations rather than an example of state welfare provision, there are moves in both England and Wales to explore and develop this model on a statutory basis. Applying the revised difference principle we can then ask whether or how this potential policy delivers in basic justice terms. On the first question of the test; whether the policy enables the social bases of effective agency, we can see from the general approach and the evaluation data that effective agency is a core aspect of this model. Through providing sustainable tenancies and person-led support rather than a staircase model of support, individuals are able to create and define their conception of the good life. One respondent in Bretherton and Pleace's (2015, p. 48) study simply stated that the main positive of the Housing First approach was that "I've got my freedom". The evaluation data shows that the majority of individuals' physical and mental health had improved through engagement with Housing First. Service users had an increased feeling of belonging where they lived, and they were in more frequent contact with family members. Importantly, the vast majority of respondents to the research stated that they felt safe most or all of the time. This is in comparison to their previous housing situation, where individuals had been homeless or rough sleeping. When we consider Maslow's hierarchy of needs, safety and health are core basic needs that individuals require before being able to exercise self-command.

Focussing on the second aspect of the test, asking whether there is a retrogressive aspect to the potential policy, we can see that there is not. Individuals who were accessing the service had been homeless for an average of 14 years prior to engaging with Housing First. In terms of meeting basic needs and enabling effective agency, we can see that this is an improvement. Although some respondents reported issues with the quality of their housing provision as well as ongoing issues with living on a limited income, in general, individuals were experiencing a safer and more supportive environment than previously. One service user in Bretherton and Pleace's (2015, p. 46) research stated:

> They've helped me no end. That's all I wanted was my own place and being settled and through their help I've got that… If you'd asked me that this time last year, everything was just chaotic and I wouldn't have thought a year down the line I'd be as settled as I am but I am, so it's all good, yes.

Evaluating this model of service provision and potential policy through my modified test shows that it enables individuals to have the social bases of effective agency. It does not diminish individuals' ability to create a conception of the good for themselves and indeed improves the ability for individuals to meet their basic needs and do and be what they want in comparison to their previous housing situation. We can clearly see the links, here, with self-command and the enabling aspect of the policy.

The final policy to explore as a means of outlining the critical capacity of the revised test is the ring-fencing of Supporting People funding in England and Wales. The Supporting People programme was created in 2003 as a ring-fenced grant of £1.8 billion to enable local authorities to fund services which help vulnerable people lead independent lives (House of Commons 2012). The focus of the funding is on housing-related support, and so services such as floating support, homelessness hostels, and supported housing can be commissioned through the funding. In England, the ring fence was removed in 2009, and both cuts to the grant and its merger into the Early Intervention, Prevention, and Support Grant occurred following the 2010 Spending Review (House of Commons 2012). This all occurred in the broad context of austerity in public services following the economic crash of 2008. Despite the changes to budget lines, the then Parliamentary Under-Secretary of State for Communities and Local Government, Sadiq Khan emphasised (Housing of Commons 2012, p. 17):

> This is the largest single grant to authorities to help millions of people live independently in their homes and this means that authorities will have the flexibility to spend this money as they see fit to help some the most vulnerable in in their communities.

We can see here the links between this policy and the revised difference principle; there is a focus on supporting the most vulnerable in society and enabling them to live independently or be effective agents.

The removal of the ring fence of this grant significantly impacted on the provision of Supporting People funding. In December 2010, Inside Housing revealed the scale of cuts in some local authorities with Nottinghamshire Council consulting on cutting 67% of its Supporting People budget (House of Commons 2012). Rochdale and Cornwall local authorities cut the use of this funding for support services by 30% and 40%, respectively. In February 2011, the Chief Executive of Homeless Link, Jenny Edwards, wrote to the Prime Minister highlighting that as much as 20% of the voluntary sector's provision for vulnerable homeless people was at risk following the removal of the ring fence. Inside Housing did further research into cuts in Supporting People funding at English councils through Freedom of Information requests in March 2012. They found that "more than 46,000 of England's most vulnerable people have had vital care services scrapped or scaled back" (House of Commons 2012, p. 21). Three hundred and five services had had money withdrawn entirely, whilst 685 services had funding reduced significantly. They noted that "Supporting People services that help homeless people, those with mental health problems, and drug and alcohol addiction are among those hit" (House of Commons 2012, p. 21). However, they did note that some councils protected budgets entirely whilst there were a range of different levels amongst those that did cut services. Finally, Capita and Inside Housing undertook a survey in July 2012 with 167 respondents. They found that 87% of services had seen a fall in funding over the last 12 months, with 38% of that being by more than half. A total of 80% of respondents had also seen an increase in the demand for Supporting People services, the majority by up to 20% (House of Commons 2012, p. 21).

When we apply the revised difference principle test to the policy of the removal of the ring fence we can see that there has been a negative impact on individuals' ability to be effective agents. As highlighted previously, the grant was intended to enable the most vulnerable in society to be able to live independently, but since the removal of the ring fence there has been a severe cut in this provision. We can suggest therefore that although the policy of removing the ring fence did not in itself fail the agency test, the consequences following this removal and the decisions made by local authorities did. In Wales, the removal of the ring fence for Supporting People funding has been proposed in the 2019/2020 draft budget. The results of the application of the test here are slightly different. This decision is being made in the context of knowledge of the impact of the removal of the ring fence in England. Decision-makers can see that the impact of this policy undermines individuals' ability to be effective agents because of the decisions often made by local authorities. In both instances, the removal of the ring fence does not enable individuals to be effective agents; however, in the English case, this does not appear to be the intention of the policy. In the Welsh case, there is clear evidence that this is the impact of implementing a removal of the ring fence. In both cases, again, there is a retrogressive impact on the most vulnerable in society in terms of effective agency. Following the cuts to services, combined with the increase need for services in the context of austerity, the support for many vulnerable individuals to lead independent lives has been removed.

In these policy examples, we can see the potential of the revised test in terms of analysing social policy according to its impact on individuals' effective agency. We can see how the test highlights policy which enables effective agency by focussing on individuals' ability to have self-command. We can also see where policy does not enable effective agency and indeed has a retrogressive impact on the most vulnerable in society. We can also draw conclusions about reasonable decision-making regarding the same policy but being implemented in different ways. If information is available on the retrogressive impact of a policy, and it is subsequently implemented, then that decision is actively undermining social justice.

Conclusion

As outlined in the introduction, this book aims to contribute to a variety of fields: housing studies, philosophy, policy, and housing practice. At its simplest, I hope it has provided another way for academics and practitioners to think hard about what is important to people. Although framed within a robust philosophical framework, the essence of the work is that everyone should have an equal opportunity to be and do what they want, and that social policy should enable this.

Within the work I have outlined a policy continuum that on one end relates to basic justice; it is to these interventions that Rawls' theory applies. I argue that measuring social justice according to only primary goods does not give us a sufficient measure of equality. Instead, we should look to the idea of effective agency to show us where and when social policy enables individuals to create a conception of the good life for themselves. The difference principle therefore provides a tool by which to measure the impact of policy interventions on basic justice; however, the metric needs to be changed to one of effective agency.

This focus on effective agency comes from Rawls' focus on individuals having two moral powers: to be reasonable and to be rational. To be rational involves being able to create a conception of the good life for oneself. This is subject to the power of reasonableness; placing limitations on individuals' actions so that others can also follow their conception of the good. The power of rationality ties to Rawls' statement that self-respect is the most important primary good. Throughout his work, Rawls focusses on individuals being free and equal, which includes the ability to create a good life for oneself. The nature of social policy as an intervention in individuals' lives demands that this is subject to tests for social justice: social policies need to be found legitimate in order to warrant the boundaries and limitations that they place on individuals' behaviour. Subsequently, there are two parts to my test for social policy. The first measures whether the social policy under scrutiny enables individuals to be effective agents. The second tests whether the social policy is retrogressive in terms of effective agency. Social policies that relate to basic justice, therefore, should have this two-part test applied to them in order to render them legitimate or not.

This specific argument is placed within the wider context of a variety of different arguments; first, that there should be a closer relationship between philosophy and the policy-making process and second, that there should be a closer engagement between normative theory and issues of housing as called for by Fitzpatrick and Watts (2018). Within this work then, I hope to have created a means by which we can apply frameworks of normative theory to policy issues, and housing policy, in particular. I have explored a number of different policy examples and suggested ways in which applying Rawls' difference principle can aid our understanding of current policy problems and responses. In the case of the 'Bedroom Tax' we have seen how this can be understood in terms of undermining effective agency through a retrogressive approach to independent living. When looking at Housing First as a policy response to homelessness, we can see how this enables individuals to create and follow a conception of the good for themselves. Finally, when looking at policy implementation in a devolved context, we can see how the test can draw out subtleties in how policy interacts with social justice dependent on information available at the time, such as in the example of Supporting People funding.

Although these ideas are discussed in this book through philosophical terminology, my test asks a relatively simple question: does this social policy enable individuals to decide what they want to do in life? When applied in the context of everyday reasoning, I suggest that there are a lot of social policies out there that fail this test. What I hope for this book, and subsequent research, to do is to present an alternative to scrutinising policy on measures such as cost-effectiveness through suggesting the metric of effective agency. If individuals are unable to exercise self-command, social policies which are imposed on individuals' lives should enable them to create an idea of the good life for themselves. If they do not do this, then something has gone wrong. If the social policy actively diminishes individuals' ability to be effective agents, then something has gone seriously wrong. The presentation of my Rawlsian framework hopefully contributes to the conversation about how we understand and scrutinise social policy, arguing for a focus on individuals' ability to do and be what they want to do and be.

Bibliography

Allen, C. (2009) 'The Fallacy of "Housing Studies": Philosophical Problems of Knowledge and Understanding in Housing Research', *Housing, Theory and Society*, 26(1), pp. 53–79.

Arneson, R.J. (1989) 'Equality and Equal Opportunity for Welfare', *Philosophical Studies: An International Journal for Philosophy in the Analytic Tradition*, 56(1), pp. 77–93.

Arneson, R.J. (1990) 'Primary Goods Reconsidered', *Noûs*, 24(3), pp. 429–454.

Arrow, K. (1973) 'Some Ordinalist-Utilitarian Notes on Rawls' Theory of Justice', *Journal of Philosophy*, 70(9), pp. 245–263.

Atkins, J. (2010) 'Moral Argument and the Justification of Policy: New Labour's Case for Welfare Reform', *The British Journal of Politics and International Relations*, 12, pp. 408–424.

Baldock, J., Manning, N., and Vickerstaff, S. (eds.) (2003) *Social Policy 2011*. Oxford: Oxford University Press.

Barry, B. (2005) *Why Social Justice Matters*. Cambridge: Polity Press.

BBC (2002) 'New Labour 'attack' under fire', *BBC News*, 11 December [Online]. Available at: http://news.bbc.co.uk/2/hi/uk_news/wales/2565859.stm (Accessed: December 2016).

Bengtsson, B. (2001) 'Housing as a Social Right: Implications for Welfare State Theory', *Scandinavian Political Studies*, 24(4), pp. 255–275.

Braybrooke, D. (1968) *Let Needs Diminish that Preferences May Flourish*. Pittsburgh: University of Pittsburgh Press.

Bretherton, J. and Pleace, N. (2015) *Housing First in England: An Evaluation of Nine Services*. York: University of York, Centre for Housing Policy.

Bretherton, J., Hunter, C., and Johnsen, S. (2013) "You Can Judge Them on How They Look...': Homelessness Officers, Medical Evidence and Decision-Making in England', *European Journal of Homelessness*, 7(1), pp. 69–92.

Butler, P. and Gentleman, A. (2014) 'Ministers Savage UN Report Calling for Abolition of UK's Bedroom Tax', *The Guardian*, 3 February [Online]. Available at: www.theguardian.com/society/2014/feb/03/ministers-savage-un-report-abolition-bedroom-tax (Accessed: September 2016).

Cairney, P. (2013) *Policy Concepts in 1000 Words: The Policy Cycle and Its Stages*. Available at: https://paulcairney.wordpress.com/2013/11/11/policy-concepts-in-1000-words-the-policy-cycle-and-its-stages/ (Accessed: January 2017).

Cameron, D. (2009) *The Big Society*, [Hugo Young Lecture]. 10 November. Available at: http://conservative-speeches.sayit.mysociety.org/speech/601246 (Accessed: September 2016).

Cameron, D. (2012) *Welfare Speech*, [Speech]. Available at: www.gov.uk/government/speeches/welfare-speech (Accessed: July 2016).

Clapham, D. (2018) 'Housing Theory, Housing Research and Housing Policy', *Housing, Theory and Society*, 35(2), pp. 163–177.

Cohen, G.A. (2000) *If You're an Egalitarian, How Come You're So Rich?* Harvard: Harvard University Press.

Conservative Party (2015) *The Conservative Party Manifesto 2015*. Available at: https://s3-eu-west-1.amazonaws.com/manifesto2015/Conservative Manifesto2015.pdf (Accessed: September 2016).

Daniels, N. (1985) *Just Health Care*. Cambridge: Cambridge University Press.

Dean, H. (2012) *Social Policy*. Cambridge: Polity.

Dewey, J. (1927) *The Public and Its Problems*. New York: Swallow.

Dworkin, R. (1981) 'What is Equality? Part 1: Equality of Welfare', *Philosophy and Public Affairs*, 10(3), pp. 185–246.

Dworkin, R. (2011) *Justice for Hedgehogs*. London: Belknap Press.

Equality and Human Rights Commission (2017) *Equality Impact Assessments*. Available at: www.equalityhumanrights.com/en/advice-and-guidance/equality-impact-assessments (Accessed:January 2017).

Fischer, F. (2000) *Citizens, Experts and the Environment*. Durham: Duke University Press.

Fitzpatrick, S. and Watts, B. (2018) 'Taking Values Seriously in Housing Studies', *Housing, Theory and Society*, 35(2), pp. 223–227.

Hall, P.A. (1993) 'Policy Paradigms, Social Learning, and the State: The Case of Economic Policymaking in Britain', *Comparative Politics*, 25(3), pp. 275–296.

Halliday, S. (2004) *Judicial Review and Compliance with Administrative Law*. Oxford: Hart Publishing.

Hanberger, A. (2003) 'Public Policy and Legitimacy: A Historical Policy Analysis of the Interplay of Public Policy and Legitimacy', *Policy Sciences*, 36(3), pp. 257–278.

Heclo, H. (1974) *Modern Social Politics in Britain and Sweden*. New Haven: Yale University Press.

Holroyd, J. (2010) 'Punishment and Justice', *Social Theory and Practice*, 36(1), pp. 78–111. Available at: www.jstor.org/stable/23558593?seq=1#page_scan_tab_contents (Accessed: December 2016).

House of Commons Library (2012) *The Supporting People Programme*. Available at: http://researchbriefings.parliament.uk/ResearchBriefing/Summary/RP12-40#fullreport (Accessed: March 2018).

Johnsen, S. (2018) *Why does Housing First Work?* Available at: https://i-sphere. org/2018/03/19/why-does-housing-first-work/ (Accessed: March 2018).

Kemeny, J. (1992) *Housing and Social Theory*. London: Routledge

King, P. (2003) 'Housing as a Freedom Right', *Housing Studies*, 18(5), pp. 661–672.

King, P. (2011) 'Using Big Ideas: The Application of Political Philosophy in Housing Research', *Housing, Theory and Society*, 28(2), pp. 109–122.

Kingdon, J.W. (1984) *Agendas, Alternatives, and Public Policies*. Boston: Little, Brown and Company.

Lipsky, M. (1971) 'Street-Level Bureaucracy and the Analysis of Urban Reform', *Urban Affairs Review*, 6, pp. 391–409.

Mandle, J. (1999) 'The Reasonable in Justice as Fairness', *Canadian Journal of Philosophy*, 29(1), pp. 75–107.

Maslow, A.H. (1943) 'A Theory of Human Motivation', *Psychological Review*, 50(4), pp. 370–396.

McKeown, S. (2008) *Housing First: A Good Practice Briefing*. Available at: http://england.shelter.org.uk/professional_resources/policy_and_research/ policy_library/policy_library_folder/housing_first_-_a_good_practice_ briefing (Accessed: March 2018).

McMahon, C. (2014) 'Rawls, Reciprocity, and the Barely Reasonable', *Utilitas*, 26(1), pp. 1–22.

McNaughton Nicholls, C. (2010) 'Housing, Homelessness and Capabilities', *Housing, Theory and Society*, 27(1), pp. 23–41. doi: 10.1080/14036090902764588.

Moller Okin, S. (1989) *Justice, Gender, and the Family*. New York: Basic Books.

Moore, M. (1996) 'On Reasonableness', *Journal of Applied Philosophy*, 13(2), pp. 167–178.

National Assembly for Wales (2014) *2014c Record of Proceedings for the National Assembly of Wales*, 24 June 2014. Available at: www.assembly.wales/ en/bus-home/pages/rop.aspx?meetingid=229#155919

Nozick, R. (1974) *Anarchy, State, and Utopia*. NewYork: Basic Books.

Nussbaum, M. (2006) *Frontiers of Justice: Disability, Nationality, Species Membership*. Harvard: Harvard University Press.

Phibbs, H. (2015) *The Spare Room Subsidy Cut Continues to Deliver Benefits*. Available at: www.conservativehome.com/localgovernment/2015/12/ the-spare-room-subsidy-cut-continues-to-deliver-benefits.html (Accessed: December 2016).

Pogge, T.W. (2004) 'The Incoherence between Rawls's Theories of Justice', *Fordham Law Review*, 72(5) [Online]. Available at: http://ir.lawnet.fordham. edu/flr/vol72/iss5/18 (Accessed: December 2016).

Power, A., et al. (2014) *The Impact of Welfare Reform on Social Landlords and Tenants*. Available at: www.jrf.org.uk/report/impact-welfare-reform-social-landlords-and-tenants (Accessed: July 2016).

Rawls, J. (1974) 'Some Reasons for the Maximin Criterion' in Freeman, S. (ed.) *John Rawls: Collected Papers*. London: Harvard University Press. pp. 225–232.

Rawls, J. (1985) 'Justice as Fairness: Political not Metaphysical', *Philosophy and Public Affairs*, 14, pp. 223–251.

Rawls, J. (1996) *Political Liberalism*. New York: Columbia University Press.

Rawls, J. (1999) *A Theory of Justice*. Harvard: Harvard University Press.

Rhodes, R.A.W. (1986) *The Natural World of Local Government*. London: George Allen and Unwin.

Roberts, P. (2007) *Political Constructivism*. London: Routledge.

Robeyns, I. (2006) 'The Capability Approach in Practice', *Journal of Political Philosophy*, 14(3), pp. 351–376.

Rolnik, R. (2013) *Report of the Special Rapporteur on Adequate Housing as a Component of the Right to an Adequate Standard of Living, and on the Right to Non-Discrimination in This Context*. Available at: www.ohchr. org/Documents/HRBodies/HRCouncil/RegularSession/Session19/A-HRC-19-53_en.pdf (Accessed: September 2016).

Ron, A. (2006) 'Rawls as a Critical Theorist: Reflective Equilibrium after the "Deliberative Turn"', *Philosophy and Social Criticism*, 32(2), pp. 173–191.

Ruonavaara, H. (2018) 'Theory of Housing, from Housing, about Housing', *Housing, Theory and Society*, 35(2), pp. 178–192.

Scanlon, T.M. (1982) 'Contractualism and Utilitarianism', in Sen, A. and Williams, B. (eds) *Utilitarianism and Beyond*. Cambridge: Cambridge University Press. pp. 103–110.

Scanlon, T.M. (2000) *What We Owe to Each Other*. Harvard: Harvard University Press.

Scanlon, T.M. (2002) 'Rawls on Justification', in Freeman, S. (ed.) *The Cambridge Companion to Rawls*. Cambridge: Cambridge University Press. pp. 139–167.

Sen, A. (1979) *The Equality of What?* Available at: www.ophi.org.uk/wp-content/uploads/Sen-1979_Equality-of-What.pdf (Accessed: July 2015).

Sen, A. (2010) *The Idea of Justice*. London: Belknap Press.

Titmuss, R.M. (1955) 'The Social Division of Welfare' in *Essays on the Welfare State*, 2nd ed. London: George Allen and Unwin. pp. 34–55.

UK Government (2012) *Welfare Reform Act 2012*. Available at: www.legislation. gov.uk/ukpga/2012/5/contents/enacted/data.htm (Accessed: July 2015).

UK Government (2012) *Welfare Reform Act 2012: Impact Assessments*. Available at: www.gov.uk/government/collections/welfare-reform-act-2012-impact-assessments (Accessed: July 2015).

Waldron, J. (1991) 'Homelessness and the Issue of Freedom', *UCLA Law Review*, 39, pp. 295–324.

Walzer, M. (1981) 'Philosophy and Democracy', *Political Theory*, 9(3), pp. 379–399.

Walzer, M. (1983) *Spheres of Justice: A Defence of Pluralism and Equality*. New York: Basic Books.

Watts, B. (2014) 'Homelessness, Empowerment and Self-Reliance in Scotland and Ireland: The Impact of Legal Rights to Housing for Homeless People', *Journal of Social Policy*, 43(4), pp. 793–810.

Wolff, J. (2011) *Ethics and Public Policy: A Philosophical Inquiry*. London: Routledge.

Wren-Lewis, S. (2013) 'Well-being as a Primary Good: Toward Legitimate Well-being Policy', *Philosophy and Public Policy Quarterly*, 31(2).

Young, S. (2008) 'Exercising Political Power Reasonably', *Critical Review of International Social and Political Philosophy*, 11(2), pp. 255–272.

Index